Harry John Wilmot-Buxton

New and contrite hearts

forty brief meditations for Lent

Harry John Wilmot-Buxton

New and contrite hearts
forty brief meditations for Lent

ISBN/EAN: 9783741193590

Manufactured in Europe, USA, Canada, Australia, Japa

Cover: Foto ©Lupo / pixelio.de

Manufactured and distributed by brebook publishing software (www.brebook.com)

Harry John Wilmot-Buxton

New and contrite hearts

New and Contrite Hearts.

I.
Ash Wednesday.

THE TURNING-POINT.

S. JOHN VI. 68.
"Lord, to whom shall we go?"

LENT is a time for asking our hearts many serious questions, and getting an honest answer. It is one of those turning-points in our life which God gives us in His mercy. As we come to Lent we come to a place where two ways meet. There is the way of the world, where men walk in the lusts of the flesh, eating and drinking, marrying, and giving in marriage; the way of Vanity Fair, with its pipe and tabor, its dance and song, its buying and selling.

Then there is the other way, God's way, the Church's way. It leads to the wilderness of temptation, it leads out of the noise and bustle of the world, it takes us to the Valley of Humiliation and the Vale of Tears, it takes us to the shadows of Gethsemane, to the Cross of Calvary. Which path shall we choose?

The world will say to us—Enjoy life while it lasts, life is

Contents.

		PAGE
I.	THE TURNING-POINT. *(Ash Wednesday)*	1
II.	SEEKING JESUS. *(Thursday after Ash Wednesday)*	5
III.	JESUS—THE WONDERFUL. *(Friday after Ash Wednesday)*	9
IV.	JESUS—THE HEALER. *(Saturday after Ash Wednesday)*	12
V.	JESUS—THE LIBERATOR. *(Monday after the First Sunday in Lent)*	16
VI.	JESUS—THE GOOD SHEPHERD. *(Tuesday after the First Sunday in Lent)*	20
VII.	GREEN PASTURES AND STILL WATERS. *(Wednesday after the First Sunday in Lent)*	23
VIII.	WANDERERS LED BACK. *(Thursday after the First Sunday in Lent)*	27
IX.	THE BRIMMING CUP. *(Friday after the First Sunday in Lent)*	30
X.	JESUS—THE REDEEMER. *(Saturday after the First Sunday in Lent)*	34
XI.	THE SHEPHERD'S VOICE. *(Monday after the Second Sunday in Lent)*	38
XII.	THE SINNER HOMELESS. *(Tuesday after the Second Sunday in Lent)*	42
XIII.	THE GOOD THINGS OF GOD. *(Wednesday after the Second Sunday in Lent)*	45
XIV.	THE WONDERFUL THINGS OF GOD. *(Thursday after the Second Sunday in Lent)*	49
XV.	THE FULL AND THE EMPTY. *(Friday after the Second Sunday in Lent)*	52
XVI.	SITTING IN DARKNESS. *(Saturday after the Second Sunday in Lent)*	56
XVII.	SELF-LOVERS. *(Monday after the Third Sunday in Lent)*	60
XVIII.	WEIGHED IN THE BALANCES. *(Tuesday after the Third Sunday in Lent)*	63

		PAGE
XIX.	THE RESPONSIBILITY OF LIFE.	
	(Wednesday after the Third Sunday in Lent)	67
XX.	THE CONSECRATED LIFE.	
	(Thursday after the Third Sunday in Lent)	71
XXI.	JACOB—A TYPE.	
	(Friday after the Third Sunday in Lent)	74
XXII.	PHARAOH—A WARNING.	
	(Saturday after the Third Sunday in Lent)	78
XXIII.	S. PETER—A WARNING TO THE IMPULSIVE.	
	(Monday after the Fourth Sunday in Lent)	82
XXIV.	PALMS AND CROSSES.	
	(Tuesday after the Fourth Sunday in Lent)	85
XXV.	THE RELIGION OF HOME.	
	(Wednesday after the Fourth Sunday in Lent)	89
XXVI.	THE RELIGION OF TRIFLES.	
	(Thursday after the Fourth Sunday in Lent)	93
XXVII.	THE RELIGION OF THE TONGUE.	
	(Friday after the Fourth Sunday in Lent)	96
XXVIII.	THE RELIGION OF EVERYDAY LIFE.	
	(Saturday after the Fourth Sunday in Lent)	100
XXIX.	THE COMFORTER.	
	(Monday after the Fifth Sunday in Lent)	103
XXX.	THE LONELINESS OF SORROW.	
	(Tuesday after the Fifth Sunday in Lent)	107
XXXI.	JUDAS AND MATTHIAS—A CONTRAST.	
	(Wednesday after the Fifth Sunday in Lent)	110
XXXII.	TRUE MANHOOD.	
	(Thursday after the Fifth Sunday in Lent)	114
XXXIII.	CRUCIFIED WITH CHRIST.	
	(Friday after the Fifth Sunday in Lent)	118
XXXIV.	BY THE CROSS.	
	(Saturday after the Fifth Sunday in Lent)	121
XXXV.	THE SEVEN WORDS.—I. *(Monday in Holy Week)*	125
XXXVI.	THE SEVEN WORDS.—II. *(Tuesday in Holy Week)*	128
XXXVII.	THE SEVEN WORDS.—III.	
	(Wednesday in Holy Week)	132
XXXVIII.	THE SEVEN WORDS.—IV., V.	
	(Thursday in Holy Week)	135
XXXIX.	THE SEVEN WORDS.—VI., VII. *(Good Friday)*	139
XL.	AT REST. *(Easter Eve)*	143

so short; eat, drink, and be merry, to-morrow we die. Yes, the old heathen world said that, a great part of the Christian world says the same. When our time of sorrow comes we shall cry out to Jesus in our distress; when the pains of death are upon us we shall ask for His rod and staff to comfort us. But what now? Shall we leave Jesus alone in His sorrows? Can we not watch with Him *one* hour? Shall He say of us, "I have trodden the wine-press alone, and of the people there was none with Me?'

Jesus speaks to each of us this Lent, and says, "Will ye also go away?" What shall our answer be? Think carefully, be sure your answer is the true one. Is this the real reply of your heart—"Lord, to whom shall we go. I will arise and go to my Father?"

Hear what God says in the Epistle of this day, "Turn ye even unto Me, saith the Lord, with all your heart, and with fasting, and with weeping, and with mourning." Is there not a cause? Can we look back over the space of time between this and last Lent without shame, without sorrow, without saying, "I am verily guilty concerning my brother; I have sinned exceedingly in thought, word, and deed?" Too many of us must feel that since last Lent we have been, like the Prodigal, away in a far country; our Father's House has been deserted, we have loved the husks of the world more than the crumbs which fall from our Heavenly Master's Table. We have grown weary of the easy yoke and the light burden, and have joined ourselves to some citizen of the world, and have found that what we thought was freedom was bitter slavery.

Well, God in His infinite mercy has given us another

season of penitence and self-examination. Once more Lent has come to us, a time when we may set our neglected house in order, when we may sweep out the dust of sloth and carelessness. And for some of us this season of grace may be the last.

There is a clock in a certain foreign town which bears this inscription in Latin—"All hours wound, but the last one kills." Every hour of our life inflicts a wound which brings us nearer to the end, and we know not when the final blow will fall. Do not let us waste this present Lent, as we perhaps have wasted many such solemn seasons gone by. How can we best use it? By trying to get away from self and nearer to Jesus.

One of the greatest stumbling blocks in the way of holiness is *self-love*. It comes to us in a thousand forms; we are all in one way or another "lovers of our own selves," and yet we profess and call ourselves followers of that Jesus Who "pleased not Himself." Well, one of the great uses of Lent is to try to conquer this self-love. We often hear it said that something which has been done to us, or said or written about us, is very *mortifying*.

We all need mortification; we are pledged in our Baptism to a life in which we must " daily mortify our evil and corrupt affections." We pray that God may kill (or mortify) all vices in us, and that all carnal affections may die in us. Now the character of the present age is specially unsuited to this life of mortification. In spite of the amount of want and misery which exists in our midst, the age, on the whole, is one of luxury. Vast sums of money are spent on personal ease and comfort, self is petted and cherished in a thousand ways. Such a state of things is a hindrance to true religion, and has been in all countries and all ages. The children of Israel in their early simple days, in their days of trouble and hard labour in Egypt, in their days of warfare and danger, lived near to God, and cried out to the Lord in their distress. When the period of ease and luxury came, when kings like Solomon wore soft raiment rather than armour, and dwelt in splendid palaces, and yielded themselves up to the influence of ease and bodily indulgence, what happened? The worship of God was neglected; idols, especially that commonest of idols—self, were put in the place of Jehovah; the country began to decline and lose its former glory. It was so with the Greeks and the Romans of old time, ease and luxury spoiled them. There is the same danger for us to-day.

The very names of the Church's Seasons have lost their significance, and to the many mean only a period of sensual self-indulgence. To the world at large, Christmas means a feast of good things, excessive eating and drinking, of giving and receiving hospitality; Shrove Tuesday points to a particular kind of food; Ash Wednesday brings no memory of the torn garments, and ashes strewn in sorrow on the head, and the solemn warning, "Dust thou art, and unto dust thou shalt return."

People love in these days to hear about enduring hardness as good soldiers of Christ, as they sit at ease in a cushioned seat, and take part in a service which must be held at the most convenient hour, and must in all points exactly suit their tastes and wishes. All this tends to a want of reality in our religion, because it involves no self-denial. Let us strive to make this Lent really useful to our souls by practising mortification some way or other. With one person it will take the form of strict fasting, with another self-denial in the matter of sleep, with another abstinence from favourite forms of reading or society.

And let us remember that in all cases the object is to keep under our bodies, to get away from self, and so to draw nearer to our Saviour Jesus. Let our prayer be—"Blessed Lord, draw me nearer to Thee by the power of Thy precious Cross, draw me away from self and self-pleasing, mortify and kill all selfish wishes and desires, that I may truly say, "Thy will, not mine, be done."

II.
Thursday after Ash Wednesday.

SEEKING JESUS.

ISAIAH LV. 6.
"Seek ye the Lord while He may be found."

OUR thoughts to-day shall be how we may approach nearer to Jesus. We are bidden over and over again to *seek* the Lord. That does not mean that Jesus is very far from any one of us, or that He purposely hides Himself. Let me show you what it does mean.

When one of those dense fogs envelopes London, or some other great city of ours, it is quite possible for us to pass our own home without being able to find it, or to walk by our dearest friend without seeing him. The home is there, the friend is there, but we cannot find them. Well, Jesus is ever close to us, a Friend ready to save to the uttermost, but we allow ourselves to be wrapped in the fog of sin, or of worldliness, and we cannot see the Lord. We fail to recognize His hand guiding our affairs; everything looks strange and distorted in the fog, and our eyes are holden so that we cannot see. How many of us are thus lost in the fog ! We are groping our way in the darkness because we do not care to walk in the True Light which lighteth every man that cometh into the world. We have let our worldly cares and business, or our worldly pleasures and amusements, wrap us up like the fog, and Jesus is shut out from our eyes.

Or take another illustration. Two persons are travelling together, walking side by side. At the end of their journey they know nothing of each other; they are as completely strangers as ever, because they have nothing in common. So there are some who have never *found* Jesus, that is, never understood Him, or His mighty love, because they have nothing in common with Him. The scholar is unable to sympathize with the man who never opens a book; the poet is uncomfortable in the society of one who sees no beauty in God's world; the pure man shrinks in horror from the talk of the filthy-minded, and the sinner can have no intercourse with Jesus, unless he has at least a wish to be a better man.

We cannot keep our sin and keep Jesus also. Yet this is what many people wish to do. They have no objection to be saved at the last from the *consequences* of their sin—
when they can commit no more evil in this world they cry

out for pardon in the world to come. They look upon the Lord Jesus as a Public Benefactor Who will save them and all men.

Let us remember, however, that Jesus does not save us *in* our sins, but *from* our sins. If a man is suffering terrible illness from excess of strong drink, you would not expect him to say to the doctor—" Save my life, but let me continue my excessive drinking." No ; we must *give up* the evil way, we must forsake the sin, we must repent us truly, we must come out of the fog, if we would draw near to Jesus.

But you tell me you cannot do this ; and I answer, " Do you *wish* to do it ; have you the *will ?* " If you have the desire to dō better Jesus will give you the means. God has given you a free will, so that you can choose life or death as you please. Jesus promises to save to the uttermost those who turn to Him, that is, those who turn *away* from their sin, and *towards* their Saviour. We must do our part, Jesus will most certainly do His ; but remember in all cases God helps those who help themselves.

Doctors sometimes tell us of patients who die simply because they do not make an effort to live. They will not co-operate with the physician, but make up their minds that they cannot recover, and so, from want of a will, they pine away and die. We sometimes hear of poor demented people who declare that they cannot move their limbs, whereas it is only the *will* to do so which is wanting.

It is often the same with the sinner. He says that he can do nothing; he cannot forsake the old foul path of sin ; all that he will do is to sit still in that evil way, and let God save him if He will. Now this is all wrong. We must have a desire for better things, and hatred, and shame, and sorrow for the evil past; like the leper, we must *want* to be clean before we can be cleansed. Like the prodigal, we must *arise* and go away from the swine-trough of the world to our Father's House; like the afflicted woman, we must struggle through the crowd of obstacles till we can touch Jesus; like the blind man, we must cast away the garment of hindrance, and arise, and come to Christ. All this means in one word—*repentance*.

The message of this Lenten season is, "Repent ye, for the Kingdom of Heaven is at hand." "If we confess our sins, He is faithful and just to forgive us our sins, and to cleanse us from all unrighteousness." Let us do our part, and leave the rest to Jesus.

Some of you, perhaps, will think that I am dwelling too much on the subject of sin. You will say to yourselves, that whilst acknowledging yourselves sinners, you cannot remember that you have committed any great wrong. We must remember, however, that sin generally—not any particular sin—is terrible to the All-Pure God, and that sin nailed Jesus Christ to the Cross.

Lives are ruined more frequently by so-called *little sins*, than by great crimes, just as houses are more frequently set on fire by a spark than a thunderbolt. We may not have committed any great sin, or what the world calls so, but still there is a heavy record against us for foolish speeches, for cruel judgments, for self-will and self-seeking, for pride, for want of charity, for slothfulness in our spiritual duties, for coldness and indifference in our prayers or our Communions. These and many like faults are the sins that do so easily beset us, which cling to us like a garment, and hinder us from coming nearer to Jesus.

Let our resolution be, by God's help, to cast away this hindering garment, this clinging, besetting sin, and let our cry be like that of the suffering folk in the Gospel—" Jesus, Thou Son of David, have mercy upon us."

III.
Friday after Ash Wednesday.

JESUS—THE WONDERFUL.

> ISAIAH IX. 6.
> "His Name shall be called Wonderful."

I HAVE said that if we desire to draw nearer to Jesus during this Lent we must cast away the garment which hinders—that is, we must repent. And this repentance must be real and sincere, not a mere dissatisfied feeling, not a mere general confession that we are sinners.

You might go on drinking impure water every day till you examined it through a microscope, then when you saw it full of poisonous matter, you would turn from it with disgust. So with our lives, unless we examine ourselves we shall never see our faults, we shall busy ourselves only with the faults of others.

One of the first duties of this season, yes, and of all seasons, is self-examination. Like the woman in the Gospel, we must light a candle, and sweep the house diligently.

Did I say *we* must light a candle? I was wrong. God must do that in answer to our prayer. "The Lord shall light my candle." He will give us the light of the Holy Spirit shining in our conscience, shining in His Word, and with that light we must examine our lives—sweep the house diligently. Our prayer must be—first, "Lord, show me *myself;*" then, "Lord, show me Thyself;" then, lastly, "Lord, make me like Thyself."

When we have seen ourselves, when we can say with the ungrateful cup-bearer of the Egyptian king, "I do remember my faults this day," then follows *contrition*, sorrow, and shame for our sins. I think if men could see the *consequences* of their sin, if they could look upon the ruined homes, the broken hearts, the blighted lives caused by their ill-doing, they would at least avoid wilful sins.

Well, we cannot know here the full fruits of our wrongdoing, but we can with the eyes of faith look on Jesus Crucified, and in that torn and mangled Body, that thorn-crowned Head, those pierced Hands and Feet, we can trace the consequences of sin. This leads to contrition. But this is only the first step to repentance. If we are sorry for our sin, we shall desire to be released from it, and to find pardon for it. Here again our will must act. If we, of our deliberate will, committed the sin, we must, by another effort of will, turn from it in repentance, and confess our fault humbly, sorrowfully, to God. And we must not stop short here. We must do our best, by God's grace, to amend our lives for the future.

Let us strive to draw near to Jesus in this spirit of repentance. He waits for us in His many-sided character of love. To-day we will think of Jesus as—The Wonderful. Ah, the many names and characteristics of Jesus are summed up in that one single word—Wonderful, which means passing knowledge, miraculous. King of kings, yet poor and despised; Teacher of love, yet hated and reviled; Prophet, yet without honour in his own country; Redeemer, yet sold to captivity; Saviour from death, yet killed by the hands of wicked men; in all, this Jesus is—The Wonderful.

Then Jesus is Wonderful in His birth. Born of a pure Virgin, conceived by the Holy Ghost, He, the Son of God, comes to His own world, which He had created, and finds no welcome, no room; angels worship Him, wise men adore Him, and the world knows Him not.

Then Jesus is Wonderful in His earthly life. He "went about doing good." "Never man spake like this Man." Whatever He touched, whatever He spoke of, became beautiful. Truly it may be said of Him, He touched nothing which He did not adorn—"Where'er He step'd a lily grew."

And Jesus is most Wonderful of all from the fact that He did all this good, and showed all this love for those who rejected Him, who laughed Him to scorn, who insulted Him, smote Him, and spit upon Him, and also put Him to a shameful death.

Now think of ourselves. This same Jesus is Wonderful in His dealings with us; wonderful in His patience, wonderful in His gentle forbearance towards our miserable tempers, our coldness, our selfishness, our want of thankfulness. Look back and recall the years that Jesus has led us through the wilderness of this world; we have rebelled against Him, we have murmured at our Leader, we have chosen our own way, we have defiled ourselves with earthly idols, and yet for all this Jesus has not left us to ourselves. The Guiding Light has shone in the darkness, the Pillar of Cloud has been our guide day by day—with what patience has Jesus suffered our manners in the desert!

O Jesu, wonderful in Thy love, wonderful in Thy long-suffering, plenteous in goodness and truth, we draw near to Thee to-day; our ingratitude, our coldness, our want of faith are wonderful, but Thy patience is more wonderful. Open our eyes that we may behold the wondrous things of Thy law; soften our hearts to understand Thy wonderful love, passing the love of women; though we come late, let it not be *too late;* of Thy wonderful mercy do away our offences.

IV.

Saturday after Ash Wednesday.

JESUS—THE HEALER.

S. JOHN V. 3.
"A great multitude of impotent folk."

HAVE you ever watched a crowd of people in the waiting-room of a hospital? If so, you will have seen "a great multitude of impotent folk," lame, maimed, blind, marked by various forms of disease and corruption, some knowing the nature of their illness, others only conscious of pain and affliction, and ignorant of the cause. And all these people are waiting with one object—to see the doctor. We are, in one sense, like those sick people. We are a multitude of impotent folk, spiritually blind, or lame, or maimed, or corrupt, and our only hope of relief and cure is to go to Jesus, the Good Physician, Who said, " They that are whole have no need of the Physician, but they that are sick ; I came not to call the righteous, but sinners to repentance."

To-day, then, we think of *Jesus as the Healer*. He it is of Whom it is written, " He hath sent Me to heal the broken-hearted, to preach deliverance unto the captives, and recovering of sight to the blind, to set at liberty them that are bruised." He it is Who has arisen, the Sun of Righteousness, with healing in His wings, and that healing comes from His own sufferings—" by His stripes we are healed."

The clever doctor in the hospital has to prescribe for all kinds of different diseases, but there are forms of illness which baffle his skill. He may be able to open the blinded eyes, to straighten the crooked limb, to free the stammering tongue, but he cannot heal the broken heart, he cannot " minister to a mind diseased," he has no balm that will soothe a wounded spirit. It is Jesus alone Who has the true medicine to heal our sickness. Our own hearts will tell us our own several needs.

Is there one here whose heart is sore with all its sense of sin, sad at the memory of lost opportunities, of blessings wasted, of innocence lost and gone ?

O sad heart, draw near to Jesus ; "a broken and a contrite heart, O Lord, Thou wilt not despise." Rend your heart, and not your garments, and turn unto the Lord your God.

O brother, sister, fellow-sinner, if our heart aches with the sense of sin, let us take our trouble to Jesus, the Healer, Who has come to bind up the broken-hearted. Is there one here whose heart is hard, so that the sense of sin causes no sorrow? One, perhaps, who is conscious of something wrong with him, who feels that his life is not all that it should be, and yet he never draws near to the Good Physician?

Have you, my brother, my sister, consulted other doctors, wasted your substance on other healers, and found no relief? Have you turned to pride, or indifference, or doubt, till your heart has grown hard and cold? These cannot help you, or give relief or comfort. Draw near to Jesus, the Healer, He alone can give a new heart, even as the heart of a little child.

There was a famous lock once, formed of rings, on which letters were engraved, and it could only be opened when the letters were so arranged as to form the name Jesus. Oh that this might be the lock of our hearts, so that they might open, not at the word gain, or honour, or riches, or pleasure, but at the one name—Jesus!

But there may be some among us who have neither the broken-hearted sorrow of the penitent sinner, nor the dissatisfied feeling of one who knows his life is wrong, and has not yet come to the Good Physician. These people are quite content with themselves, and see no necessity for observing Lent or any other season with special care. These are the blind people, "eyes have they, but they see not." It is truly said there are none so blind as those who will not see. We pity those who *cannot* see;

what shall we say of those who *will not* see? Self-blindness is the saddest, as it is the commonest, of diseases. O Lord, show me *myself,* then I shall know my need of Thee; then I shall cry—O Lord, show me *Thyself,* open mine eyes, that I sleep not in death.

And if we draw nigh to Jesus, the Healer, what medicine will He give us to heal our sickness? It must needs be bitter to our taste. "By His stripes we are healed;" we must be partakers of His sufferings if we are to receive the fruit of them. Shall we leave all the gall and vinegar to Jesus whilst we eat of the fat and drink of the strong; shall the cup of agony be His, and the cup of this world's pleasure ours? No, we must not shrink from the bitter medicine of repentance, the myrrh of self-denial. Sometimes the surgeon can only cure a patient by cutting off the diseased part with the keen steel; so Jesus, the Healer, bids us pluck out the offending eye, or cut off the offending hand, since it is better to enter into life blind or maimed, than having two eyes or two hands, to perish. It is sometimes necessary for the surgeon to break the bones of a patient to prevent him being a cripple for life, so when Jesus in His mercy breaks our bones with the rod of sorrow and chastisement, let our cry be that of penitent David—" Make me to hear joy and gladness, that the bones which Thou hast broken may rejoice."

O Jesus, Thou Healer of the sick, we impotent folk draw near to-day, bringing our sins and our sorrows, our weakness and our faults, our broken resolutions, our many failures; speak the word only, and Thy servants shall be made whole.

V.

Monday after the First Sunday in Lent.

JESUS—THE LIBERATOR.

PSALM CXLVI. 7 *(Prayer Book Version)*.
"The Lord looseth me out of prison."

LIBERTY—a free country! Those are words dear to us all. We love and honour the memory of those who in the old days fought for England's freedom. We read with pride of the Swiss hero who flung himself upon the Austrian spears, and made a way for liberty. But what shall we say of Jesus, Who gives us the truest liberty, Whose service is *perfect* freedom, Who loosest men out of prison?

There are few words which have been more misused than that word liberty. Well might the French woman, victim of the Revolution, point to the Statue of Freedom, as she came to die upon the scaffold, and say, "O Liberty, how many crimes have been committed in thy name."

"Truly," says one of our great preachers, "there are two freedoms—the false, where a man is free to do what he *likes;* the true, where a man is free to do what *he ought.*"

Never mistake license for liberty. The truest freedom is that of the Christian who is *not* free to do wrong. The man who keeps a guard over himself, who keeps his mouth as it were with a bridle, who keeps under his body, who controls his temper, this man is free; free from the stings of an accusing conscience, free from the bitter pangs of remorse, free from the restless, unsatisfied doubts and fears of the ungodly, he possesses that peace which the world cannot give.

It is especially the mistake of the young to imagine that to have one's own way means liberty and happiness. The Prodigal, starting from his father's house, talks gaily of his freedom, of being his own master; he soon finds that he is a prisoner, fast bound in the misery and iron of evil habits, unholy desires, selfish pleasures, bad company. He is no less a prisoner because he has locked the door upon himself.

Look at the drunkard, or the unclean, or the passionate, or the unbeliever; ask him if he is free, if he is happy, and he will answer you, if he speaks truly, " Alas, I am so fast in prison that I cannot get forth."

Once they were shouting in the streets of Paris—Liberty, equality, brotherhood. What did they mean?—Cruelty, oppression, murder.

But, as says one truly, those names belong to the Christian, his Bible tells him of his freedom, his Baptism proclaims his equality, the Blessed Sacrament of the Altar his brotherhood.

"The Lord looseth men out of prison." He looseth out of the hard prison of the ancient law, and setteth our feet in the large room of grace, and bringeth us into a wealthy place. He looseth out of the prison of sin and death, the prison of the curse. He Who went down into Hades, and preached to the spirits of the Fathers in prison, hath broken for us the gates of brass, and smitten the bars of iron in sunder. Death can put no seal upon our tomb which shall keep us prisoners there. The seal is broken, the stone is rolled away; because He lives, we shall live also; the Lord looseth me out of prison. And yet for all this, some of us are conscious that we are prisoners, tied and bound with the chain of our sins. There is one doubtful and troubled about many things. Such an one is a prisoner in a dark cell. Anxiety hangs like a chain about him. All is gloomy with him, let God's blessed sun shine ever so brightly. To-morrow, next year, the future, these are ever in his thoughts.

My brother, my sister, ask Jesus, the Liberator, to set you free, to loose you out of this dark prison, to give you faith, trust, hope, *peace in believing*.

Are you the slave of an undisciplined temper, free, as you fancy, to say what you will, no matter how your words vex or wound? Oh, ask Jesus to open the door, to loose you out of that most wretched of condemned cells. Your own life, that of those around you, must be miserable if you cannot control yourself. I know of no existence more utterly miserable than to be constantly exposed to an undisciplined temper. Jesus, the meek and gentle, Jesus, Who opened not his mouth, Jesus, the Liberator, can alone loose you out of that prison. God and your own heart alone know the secrets of your prison-house.

The criminal condemned to gaol bears the marks of his punishment about him, his dress, his appearance point him out for what he is. But it is not so with the sinner against God. To the eyes of the world he appears a free man. Look at one who is the darling of society, occupying a place of rank and importance. Men and women seek his company, and delight to do him honour. Yet the man is a prisoner. He goes home at night from the brilliant assembly, to his prison cell. He is shut up alone with conscience—his gaoler. He is the prisoner of impure thoughts and deeds. Nothing is pure to him, and remorse, like a chain, eats into him. So it is with every unpardoned sinner.

Are there none of us who are prisoners—captives and slaves to our own bad passions, our own undisciplined will, evil habits of our own making? If so, and if we have the will to be free, Jesus, the Liberator, will loose us, even though we be in the innermost prison of sin, and our feet made fast in the stocks of evil habits.

But we shall never be free till we know that we are in prison, till we feel the chain. The young man following his own lusts and pleasures, walking in his own way, talks to us of his freedom; he knows not that he is a prisoner, and so he will not cry to the Lord to set him free.

If I speak to a poor mad prisoner in his asylum, he will assure me that he is quite sane, and at liberty, whereas *I* am mad, and in prison. So it is with the captive in the prison-house of sin, he tells me he is his own master.

We are too apt to call things by their wrong names. In some parts of England they call the wild clematis *honest wood*, a pretty name, but not a true one. The plant has so grown and increased that it destroys hazel, thorn, and maple. Every hedge is choked with it. So we like to call our vices by the name of pleasures, our sins by the title of our weaknesses, and our slavery to evil by the flattering misused word—liberty.

My brother, my sister, do you feel the chain, would you be loosed out of prison? Then let your prayer be—Blessed Jesus, Who camest to preach deliverance to the captives, give us holy freedom, open the prison, strike off these binding chains, lead us forth into the land of righteousness, for Thy Name's sake.

VI.

Tuesday after the First Sunday in Lent.

JESUS—THE GOOD SHEPHERD.

PSALM XXIII. 1.
"The Lord is my Shepherd."

ALL the Psalms are precious to God's people, but none more so than this Psalm of the Good Shepherd. It is dear to us from old associations, for most of us learnt it by heart in our childhood, when we wore the white flower of innocency. It is dear to us as bringing peace and comfort at our last hour, for when we enter the Valley of the Shadow of Death we love to hear that the Shepherd is with us, and that His rod and staff comfort us.

Among all the titles which belong to the Name that is above every name, none appeals to our heart more than that of the Good Shepherd. It is just because we are so weak, so timid, so easily led astray, that we love to think of Jesus as our *Shepherd*, One Who leads His sheep, and tenderly carries those who are too feeble to follow Him, and Who seeks diligently for those who have strayed until He finds them, and rejoices over His poor wanderer when he is brought home. We know that we have all erred and strayed from God's way like lost sheep. We know that in this world we are sent forth as sheep in the midst of wolves. But we know more than this, that Jesus, the Good Shepherd, is *our* Shepherd, that He knows His sheep, that He has laid down His life for them, and that therefore they are very precious in His sight.

Blessed are they who have this faith, who can say under all circumstances, "The Lord is *my* Shepherd, therefore can I lack nothing." The unbelieving world is always in want, always seeking something, and never satisfied; the Christian can say, "I have learned in whatsoever state I am therewith to be content—the Lord is my Shepherd, therefore can I lack *nothing*."

Those who have left this world and entered into rest can see their Shepherd face to face; there He leads His flock, His beautiful flock, upon the Celestial Mountains; we are yet in the wilderness of this world, some of us have wandered over the dark mountains of temptation, but Jesus is our Shepherd also. He delivers us from the hand of the enemy, from Satan, the roaring lion, who goeth about to devour us.

Because Jesus is our Shepherd we can lack nothing, "No good thing will He withhold from them that walk uprightly." To supply all our needs Jesus lacked everything—home, food, friendship, love. There was no room for Him in the inn, He had not where to lay His head, yet He gives us room in His Holy Church, and we can say, "I will lay me down and take my rest, for it is Thou, Lord, only, Who makest me to dwell in safety." He was an hungered, and thirsted by the well, but He fills us with the finest wheat flour, and with honey out of the stony rock. He was without bread in the wilderness, but for us there is the Bread of Heaven here in the wilderness of this world, for us there is the pure Water of Life, flowing in the Sacraments from the Rock of Ages cleft for us, and whosoever drinketh of this water shall never thirst.

No, we can lack nothing; we may lack money, but though silver and gold have we none, we have that peace which the world cannot give, which money cannot buy. God's promises are dearer to us than thousands of gold and silver. We may lack worldly position, and be despised and rejected of men; then we shall be more like Jesus our Shepherd; the world knew Him not, and despised Him; for us it is better to be unknown to the world, and well known to Him Who knows His sheep, and is known of them. For our part we would rather be door-keepers in the House of the Lord than dwell in the tents of ungodliness. We may lack health and strength, but we shall gain more than we lose. We shall know that we are partakers of the sufferings of Jesus, that our sick-bed is our cross, whereon we are crucified with Christ; our throbbing head will remind us that we are permitted to wear the thorny crown as He did; that we too are allowed to drink of the cup of sorrow which He drank, and we are cheered by the promise that if we suffer with Him we shall be glorified with Him. We may lack earthly friends, but we have the friendship of Him Who sticketh closer than a brother, Who says, "I will never leave you, nor forsake you." A Friend whose whole thoughts are for us and none for self; a Friend Who bears with our folly and our evil temper, Who is patient and long-suffering, Who never wearies of us, Who cannot be taken from us by separation or by death.

When we, a timid, feeble flock, pass through the waters of trouble, Jesus, the Good Shepherd, is with us; we may sink in the deep waters, "but they shall not go even over our soul." When we pass through the fire of temptation, Jesus is with us; in the fiery furnace of trial is One like unto the Son of God. Wherever we, the sheep, are called upon to go, Jesus, the Shepherd, has been before us. In the battle we are called on to fight, Jesus has fought and conquered; in the struggle between self-will and God's will, Jesus has taken part and triumphed; if the cross is laid upon us, Jesus has borne it before us; if we come to die, Jesus has died, and taken away the sting of death; and now He giveth to His beloved while they sleep.

Blessed Jesus, Thou Great Shepherd of the sheep, lead us, Thy flock, in the paths of righteousness, bear tenderly with our weakness and our faults, keep us in the true Fold of Thy Church, lead us by the green pastures and still waters of comfort, for Thy Name's sake.

VII.

Wednesday after the First Sunday in Lent.

GREEN PASTURES AND STILL WATERS.

PSALM XXIII. 2 *(Prayer Book Version).*
"He shall feed me in a green pasture, and lead me forth beside the waters of comfort."

THIS promise is full of restfulness, peace, joy. The man who knows not God, and cares not for religion, is a wanderer in a barren and dry land, where no water is. The man who goes on in his sin, unrepentant and unforgiven, knows nothing of the meaning of those sweet words—comfort, rest. Well says the Scripture, "The ungodly are like the troubled sea; there is no peace, saith my God, for the wicked."

We are shown in the Gospels that those possessed by evil spirits were restless, wandering to and fro, seeking rest and finding none. This restlessness, this unsatisfied longing, is ever a mark of those who have not come to Jesus and found rest for their souls. For them life is the barren and dry land; for those who have drawn near to Jesus life is the green pasture, the water of comfort.

Travellers in the desert tell us that when the eye is weary and pained with the glare of the sun upon the dry sand, nothing is so refreshing as the sight of a green spot, an oasis in the wilderness. So to the sinner who has wandered out of the way in the wilderness of this life, whose eyes are wearied with the glare of the world, precious indeed are the green pastures and the still waters which he finds when he has turned in repentance to the Good Shepherd.

And what, then, must we understand by these green pastures? Surely we see in them the Holy Church. The green spot in the midst of the desert of the world, a desert choked with the sand of selfishness, and strewn with the bones of those who have perished out of the way. Outside in the sinful world there are the heat and the glare, and the weary toil for that which is not bread. Here in the Church is the green pasture where the flock may feed and rest in peace; here the Good Shepherd feeds His sheep, so that they shall hunger no more, neither thirst any more, except after righteousness; here He knows His sheep and calls them all by their names.

These pastures of Christ's Church are ever green, because they are watered by the dew of the Holy Spirit, and those that rest among them shall be as trees planted by the waterside, their leaf shall not wither, the sun shall not burn them by day, neither the moon by night. Well may we cry—

> "Faithful Shepherd, feed me
> In the pastures green;
> Faithful Shepherd, lead me
> Where Thy steps are seen."

But it is not only of the Church on earth that we must think when speaking of the green pastures. "There remaineth a rest for the people of God." "Beyond these voices" are the green pastures of Paradise, where the Saints of God rest from their labours, where the sheep never wander, and the wolf draws not nigh the fold.

The Church on earth and the Church in Paradise is all one. The Kingdom of Heaven and the green pastures stretch away in ever-brightening verdure beyond the grave and into the fairer world above.

"He shall lead me beside the waters of comfort." Many are the meanings which pious minds have found in these words, all true, all beautiful. In the waters of comfort we see the holy water of Baptism, and Jesus the Good Shepherd taking the tender lambs of the flock, and washing them white, and saying, "I will, be thou clean." In these waters of comfort we see the streams of grace ever flowing in the Church through her Sacraments and Ordinances; a precious healing pool, better than that of Siloam, where the weak are made strong, where the blind see, and the lame walk, and the lepers are cleansed. These waters are the river of the water of life, clear as crystal, proceeding out of the Throne of God, and of the Lamb, flowing from the Church above to the Church below.

It is by these waters of comfort that the Good Shepherd leads us; as tender lambs He carries us in His arms, as young men and maidens He guides us with His rod, as old and feeble He supports us with His staff; but always by the waters of comfort.

And again, we see in those waters the image of the Holy Scripture. "As cold water to a thirsty soul, so is good news from a far country." We who hunger and thirst after righteousness can drink out of the wells of salvation, and the good news from a far country, the Gospel of the Blessed God, shall be to us as living waters. By patience, and comfort of God's Holy Word, we shall embrace and ever hold fast the blessed hope of everlasting life which has been given us in our Saviour Jesus Christ.

Blessed Jesus, Tender Shepherd, we have erred and strayed from Thy ways like lost sheep; pardon our wanderings in thought, word, and deed, carry us out of the wilderness of sin and danger, heal our poor bruised hearts, absolve us from our offences, and set us once more in Thy green pastures, and lead us beside the waters of comfort.

VIII.
Thursday after the First Sunday in Lent.

WANDERERS LED BACK.

Psalm XXIII. 3.
"He shall convert my soul, and bring me forth in the paths of righteousness, for His Name's sake."

"TURN thou us, O good Lord, and so shall we be turned." Such should be our Lenten prayer. The Lord only can turn us from evil to good, from the wrong way to the right. We, indeed, must follow His leading, must yield to His guiding, but it is He Who turned the water into wine, Who alone can turn us from sin unto righteousness. We have His promise that He will *convert* our soul, that is, turn us back from the wrong way.

Few words have been more misapplied and mistaken than the word *conversion*. To many, the very term is offensive, simply because it has been vulgarized and misused. Yet conversion, in its true sense, is a very solemn fact, and a real necessity for all. Who is there who has not fallen into sin after Baptism? With some it is a sin of wilfulness, with others it is a sin of weakness or ignorance, with very many the fault is one of neglect and omission. In any case, we have wandered from the right way, and we need to be turned back to it. This is conversion, this is the work of God, this is the loving ministry of the Good Shepherd—to bring back the wandering sheep.

This conversion *may* be sudden, just as we may pluck a man back from the edge of a precipice, but it is usually a gradual work. There are certain kinds of palms whose buds open suddenly, and with a noise which echoes through the forest; but most buds open gradually and in silence. So there are some who are turned back to God suddenly, amid the noise of the earthquake, the fire, or the mighty rushing wind. But with most the conversion—the turning back—is gradual, as the soul hearkens to the still small voice.

Have you seen a loving mother finding a wandering child who has lost its way? There is the kiss of love to restore confidence and hope to the wanderer, there is the ready hand to guide and support the feeble feet, step by step, on the road home. So God deals with us. It is the *love* of Jesus, the Good Shepherd, which draws us back to the fold—it is His hand which guides our poor faltering steps along the right way.

And see, He brings us forth into the paths of righteousness. Not the paths of the old hard law in which a man could not walk without tripping, but in that path which Jesus Himself has trodden, so that we may follow the steps of His most holy life, Who fulfilled all righteousness. One of old said, "No one can go wrong on a straight road." Such is the road along which the Good Shepherd leads us.

We are all very like children learning to walk. We are bidden to go forward, we are expected each day to make some progress, we are bidden day by day to go up higher. Like children, we shall often fall, often turn aside ; but if we are *loving* children we shall ask for help, we shall cling to the guiding hand, we shall go forward, though it be but feebly.

Do not be discouraged, dear brethren, at the thought of the little seeming progress which you make. You *are* making progress if you are trying daily to get the better of your sin, to trample down one evil habit. Humility—dissatisfaction with our spiritual state—is a sure sign that we are being converted. Nothing is more fatal than the self-satisfied condition of the mistaken people who declare that they are converted, and that, therefore, there remains nothing for them but the contemplation of their own self-righteousness.

True conversion will make us lowly, distrustful of self, ready, with holy Paul, to call ourselves the chief of sinners, and anxious to walk *humbly* with our God. Our cry will be—

> "I am weak, but Thou art mighty,
> Hold me with Thy powerful hand."

And that powerful, yet gentle, hand will lead us through the paths of righteousness till we leave this life, and when we pass through the valley of the shadow of death we shall fear no evil, for the Good Shepherd will still be with us. How full is that promise, "I will never leave thee, nor forsake thee!"

When we come to the last journey others must be left. They can only stand on this side and look longingly, we must journey on without them, and yet not alone, for Jesus is with us, His rod and staff comfort us. And notice here, that the valley is called the valley of the *shadow* of death—not that of black darkness. Jesus, the Sun of Righteousness, has passed through it, and the clouds have been broken before His brightness. For the Christian, death is but a passage through the twilight, through the shadow unto the perfect day.

In one sense, however, all our life is a journey through the valley of the shadow of death. Sorrow, loss, trial, cast their shadows over our path. But what then, we can say with truth, "I will fear no evil."

I have heard that said by a poor lonely old cottager, who had no earthly friends to care for him, who seemed to have nothing, and yet possessed all things.

Yea, the darkness is no darkness to us, the night of sorrow is as clear as the day. His rod and His staff comfort us. The rod chastens us for our foolishness, the staff supports our feeble limbs. Let us kiss the rod, let us clasp the staff.

Blessed Jesus, turn us back to the right way, lead us into the paths of righteousness; in the valley of the shadow of sorrow, of pain, of death, be with us, give us the comfort of Thy rod and staff, and we shall fear no evil.

IX.

Friday after the First Sunday in Lent.

THE BRIMMING CUP.

PSALM XXIII. 5.
"My cup runneth over."

WHERE shall we look for this cup? Surely in the hand of Jesus, the Good Shepherd. "In the hand of the Lord there is a cup, and the wine is red." Yes, it is the precious wine of a Saviour's Blood, shed to cleanse us from all sin. The Psalm tells us, also, where we must receive that cup of blessing: "Thou shalt prepare a table for me against them that trouble me." We know that table is the Altar of our Lord, where the great feast of good things is prepared for us. There we shall find food, strength, shelter from those that trouble us.

Alas, how many they are! Our sins ever trouble us; of them we may say, "Mine enemies live and are mighty." Satan, our enemy, troubles us, he desires to have us that he may sift us like wheat, and specially those who are trying to lead holy lives. Our sorrows, and losses, and worries trouble us; and against all these enemies the Lord has prepared for us a place to hide us in, from the strife of tongues and the provoking of all men.

The world, the flesh, the devil, set forth their tables in our sight; they tempt us with a thousand delicacies, a thousand glittering baits; they say to us, "Come, eat of the sweet, and drink of the strong. Life is short, let it be merry, gather you roses while you may." So they offer us the intoxicating cup of worldly pleasure, the highly-spiced food of dissipation, that sweet morsel—*our own way*. But the warning comes to us, "In the day that ye eat thereof ye shall surely die!" If we feed at the feast of sin, we shall be like the guests of the cruel Borgias, whose food and wine were poisoned, and brought death.

Against these enemies the Lord hath prepared for us a Table, and if there we eat of that bread and drink of that cup, we shall not fear what man can do unto us. Our enemies will continue to trouble us as long as we are here in a strange land; as strangers and pilgrims, we shall find that we are in the midst of foes. But in the Blessed Food of the Altar we shall gain help, and in the strength of that Food we shall go on to Horeb, the Heavenly Mount of God.

"Thou hast anointed my head with oil." Yes, we, who have been confirmed and admitted to Holy Communion through that gate of Confirmation, can say this. We have been anointed with the Holy Ghost, we have an unction from the Holy One. We have been anointed with the oil of the Holy Spirit, which maketh our faces to shine with joy and gladness.

"And our cup runneth over." Our cup of Salvation runneth over; Jesus has done, is doing, for us more than we have desired or deserved. Our cup of blessings runneth over. Think how good God has been to us ever since we were born; think of last year and its mercies. We have slept in careless indifference, and God has watched over us as a parent over a slumbering child. We have been wayward, peevish, discontented, ungrateful, yet God has borne with us. He has never failed to give us good things, though we may have forgotten to be thankful.

Some of us have known many sorrows—we feel that our cup of suffering has been filled over and over again. Well, "the cup that our Father hath given us, shall we not drink it?" Is not that very bitter cup a cup of blessing? Cannot we say with David, "Before I was troubled I went wrong?" When that cup of sorrow is given to us, let us remember Gethsemane, and our Master's agony. His cup of sorrow was drunk there, and again at cruel Calvary, before there came the glorious Resurrection and Ascension. Welcome the bitter cup, welcome the wormwood and the gall, if they bring us nearer to Jesus.

Do you know how the pearls are formed in the oyster? Some foreign and irritating substance enters the oyster's shell, and the oyster covers it with layers of pearl, so that what was a painful and troublesome thing becomes a jewel of great price. So by God's grace we may make our sorrows into blessings, and by bearing them with patience, gentleness, and meekness, change this irritating trouble into a precious pearl for our everlasting crown.

"Thy lovingkindness and mercy shall follow me all the days of my life, and I will dwell in the House of the Lord for ever!" Here is the blessed assurance that the Lord will never leave us, nor forsake us. Here is the promise that he that endureth unto the end shall be saved. So we may cry—

"'Tis mine, 'tis mine, that country,
If I but persevere."

Ah! what need we have to pray for that grace of perseverance! So many of us are like the seed on the rocky ground; we grow up quickly, and as quickly wither away, because we have *no root*. One day we are full of zeal, full of high aims and good resolutions, but the next we have looked back, and taken our hand from the plough; we came running to Jesus, like the young ruler, now we have gone sadly away from Him. Let our prayer be for grace to persevere, to remain steadfast unto the end. The lovingkindness of the Lord endureth yet daily; His grace is before us to clear our path of dangers and difficulties, it follows after us to keep us in the way, to urge us on our course.

"I will dwell in the House of the Lord for ever." Here for a little while on earth we can say, "I was glad when they said unto me, We will go into the House of the Lord. I love the place, O Lord, wherein Thine honour dwells." Here for a little while we can find a resting-place for our weary souls at Thy Altar, O Lord of Hosts. Here for a little while we shall find our greatest happiness in the Services of the Sanctuary. And then, after we are delivered from the burden of the flesh, we shall dwell in the House of the Lord, the House not made with hands, eternal in the Heavens.

Blessed Jesu, my Shepherd and my Friend, my cup of thankfulness runneth over, I thank Thee for my joys, I thank thee for my sorrows, blessings alike; let not mine enemies triumph over, let Thy grace always prevent me and follow me, and grant me, with the residue of Thy Holy Church, to dwell in Thy House for ever.

X.

Saturday after the First Sunday in Lent.

JESUS—THE REDEEMER.

PSALM CVII. 2 *(Prayer Book Version).*
"Let them give thanks whom the Lord hath redeemed, and delivered from the hand of the enemy."

THE life and wanderings of God's people Israel of old find a parallel in the life and wanderings of God's Spiritual

Israel now. For us there is the wilderness of this world, a place of danger, of toil, of weariness, through which lies the path to the Promised Land. For us, as for Israel, there are enemies to be encountered, dangers to be met, temptations to be endured. For us, also, as for them, there are graves of lust, memorials of our grievous sin, there is some Taberah—some *Burning*, where the Lord sent the fire of affliction upon us ; and also, thanks be to God, there are green spots of rest and refreshment, like Elim—spots where we find a hiding-place from the wind, and a covert from the tempest, and the shadow of a great rock in a weary land.

And in all our wanderings here, Jesus, the Good Shepherd, Jesus, the Redeemer, is with us. The brethren of David asked him in scorn, "With whom hast thou left those few sheep in the wilderness?" That question may not be asked of David's Greater Son, for here in the wilderness the Lord Himself leads us like a flock, and says to us, " Fear not, little flock ; for it is your Father's good pleasure to give you the kingdom." To give to *us* the kingdom—to us, who have erred and strayed like lost sheep, who have followed the devices and desires of our own hearts ! O marvellous love of Jesus, Who has carried the strayed sheep home again, and Who says, " Rejoice with Me, for I have found My sheep which was lost."

Jesus, then, is with us in the wilderness; in temptation, in trial, in hardship, in affliction, Jesus is with us ; of whom then shall we be afraid ? Hear what He says to us—"I am the Good Shepherd, and know My sheep, and am known of Mine."

When Jesus, the Good Shepherd, died on the Cross,

laying down His life for the sheep, He did not do this for mankind as a whole, but for men as individuals; He died, as it were, with the name of each upon His lips. As the dying father calls his sons by name to his bedside to receive his last blessing, and his last counsel, so Jesus on the Cross dies calling sinners to Him *by name*. Think of this when next you kneel at the Altar to receive the Holy Eucharist, then you will find new force in those words, spoken to each of you—" The Body of Christ which was given for *thee*. Drink this in remembrance that Christ's Blood was shed for *thee*, and be thankful."

And now in Heaven, before the Throne, Jesus, our Great High Priest, mentions us by name in His great work of intercession; He pleads for us by name, and bears our names upon His heart, even as Aaron bore upon his breastplate the names of the tribes of Israel.

" I know My sheep." Yes, Thou God knowest my weakness, my sin, my folly. Thou knowest how easily I go wrong, how ready I am to yield to temptation, how feeble my purposes. Thou knowest how often I make good resolves and break them, how frequently I sin with my tongue, and speak unadvisedly with my lips, how constantly my rebellious will fights against duty, how often the good that I would I do not, and the evil that I would not, that I do. Thou knowest the very secrets of my heart; to Thee all hearts be open, all desires known; Thou knowest, I trust, that I want to keep in the narrow way, that I want to bear my cross with patience, and fight my battle with endurance; Thou knowest—O dare I say so—Thou knowest that I love Thee.

Let this thought comfort us—"I know My sheep." Jesus understands all our wants and weaknesses. He knows exactly how heavy a cross we are able to bear, exactly how strong a temptation we can endure. In the old evil days of torture, the sentence on some unhappy criminal was that there should be laid upon him as great a weight of stone or iron as he could bear, *and more*.

Jesus never lays on us a greater burden than we can, with His help, sustain. He tells us that He not only knows His sheep, but is known of them. There must be an answering knowledge, a return of affection. The child understands the parent who loves it, the animal responds to the caress of its owner.

But can we attain to this—to know the love of Christ which passeth knowledge? Not perfectly here on earth, for here we see as in a glass, darkly—we know in part. But yet we can know something of Christ. We can know something of the blessedness of Absolution, when we feel our sins are forgiven us; we can know something of the joy of hope, when we go forward and press towards the mark; we can know something of the strength of faith, when we pray, casting all our care upon Him, and knowing that He careth for us; we can know something of the love of Christ when He comes to us in the Blessed Sacrament, healing, cleansing, strengthening, comforting our souls. And this knowledge of Christ is not the knowledge of books, or of learning, it is not the knowing *about* Christ which we need, but the knowing *Christ*. "The secret of the Lord is with them that fear Him."

Have you ever noticed how two children who love one

another have their little secret pleasures into which others cannot enter? So it is with those who fear the Lord Jesus, He and His sheep understand one another. There is a secret bond of union between them which the world cannot comprehend.

Blessed Jesu, Who hast redeemed me, and called me by my Christian name, that I might be Thine own child by adoption, ever plead for me by name, let me know one day even as I am known; O Thou, Whose Name is above every name, let my poor name be written in the Lamb's Book of Life.

XI.

Monday after the Second Sunday in Lent.

THE SHEPHERD'S VOICE.

S. JOHN x. 3.
"The sheep hear His voice."

THE pride and folly of man brought confusion into the world and created Babel. Since then the earth has been filled with different languages, all mainly employed in talking of self. Jesus came to make all men one, to unite in one family all the kindreds of the earth. So now, wherever men hold the Catholic Faith their speech is one, no matter what their country. They are united by one Faith, one Baptism, one hope of their calling, one Lord and Father of all.

I have read how a Hindu and a New Zealander, who had

been converted to Christianity, met on board a Missionary ship. Neither understood the language of the other, yet as Christians they had a speech in common—the one said "Alleluia!" the other answered, "Amen."

Jesus has gathered His sheep out of all lands—from the East, from the West, from the North, and from the South—a great multitude, which no man can number, of all nations and kindreds, and peoples, and tongues. Men have dreamed of a universal language, and have vainly tried to invent it; but the Christian has indeed a language common to all who believe—the language of love, the voice of Jesus. That voice of the Good Shepherd is ever speaking to us: have we heard, have we understood, have we obeyed?

In our great cities the sound of the Church-going bell, or the voice of the teacher, are drowned by the roar and clatter of the busy streets. So there is the great danger of allowing the voices of the world to stifle and overcome the voice of Jesus. There are many voices ringing in our ears; the loud laugh of pleasure, the deep groaning of the discontented, the eager voice of greed and selfishness are all around us. We must not let this worldly din drown the voice of the Good Shepherd.

> "O let me hear Thee speaking,
> In accents clear and still,
> Above the storms of passion,
> The murmurs of self-will;
> O, speak to reassure me,
> To hasten, or control,
> O speak, and make me listen,
> Thou Guardian of my soul."

Jesus speaks to us in love, in pity, in warning. He speaks

in love, and says to us, "I am come that they might have life, and that they might have it more abundantly. Whomsoever cometh unto Me, I will in no wise cast out." He speaks in pity, and says to us, "There is joy in the presence of the Angels of God over one sinner that repenteth. Though your sins be as scarlet, they shall be white as snow. Come unto Me, all ye that travail and are heavy laden, and I will refresh you." He speaks to us in warning, and tells us that those who now reject Him as a Saviour, shall one day tremble before Him as a Judge. He tells us how the Great White Throne shall be set, and the books of Judgment opened, and that then the false and the true shall be separated, and the sheep shall be on the Shepherd's right hand, and the goats on His left.

Have we hearkened unto the voice of the Good Shepherd? He spoke to us in the time of our tribulation, when the windows were darkened, and the shadow of death had fallen, and He whispered, "I am the Resurrection and the Life; he that believeth in Me shall never die." He spoke to us in the time of our illness, when we lay watchful through the long night, and heard "the rain upon the roof." He spoke to us in love, bidding us call our sins to remembrance, and telling us how He is the Good Physician, Who can heal our diseases. He spoke to us in the time of our prosperity, when once more all things smiled upon us, and He warned us not to set our affections on things below, where the rust and moth do corrupt, but on things above.

In every event of our lives, in our dark days, and our days of brightness, in the time of tears and of laughter, the voice of the Good Shepherd has spoken. He spoke to us in our innocent childhood, in our tempted youth, in our busy maturity—have we listened, have we answered? Day by day the voice of the Good Shepherd speaks to us from Heaven, saying, " Come up hither—Friend, go up higher." At times that voice speaks to us as it were from the Cross. Some bitter struggle has to be gone through ; the conflict between God's will and our will has to be fought ; we have to make a sacrifice ; then the voice of Jesus speaks and reminds us of His Cross and agony, His perfect sacrifice of self, and reminds us that we must be partakers of His sufferings if we are to share in His glory.

It may be that we have often disregarded the loving tones, the pleading accents, the warning notes of that voice. It is a sad thing to remember, as we stand at our mother's grave, that we would not listen to the gentle teaching of her whose voice on earth is still for ever. Still more sad is it to know that we would not listen to the voice of Jesus, Who loves us, and gave Himself for us. If we have wandered, if we have turned a deaf ear to the Shepherd's voice, let us return, let us go to our Lord right humbly. See ! He calls us to Him ; He gives us another chance ; He says, *"Begin again !"*

> " Child, hast thou deeply sinned,
> Lost thy baptismal grace ?
> Go, seek the Great High Priest,
> With tears His feet embrace ;
> O hear His pitying voice—
> ' I pardon thee, rejoice ;
> With cleansing blood bedewed,
> With health and peace renewed—
> Begin again.' "

Blessed Jesu, we have turned from Thy loving call, and been often deaf to Thy voice. O forsake us not utterly, neither take Thy Holy Spirit from us. Open our dull ears to hearken; speak to us again in mercy and love; forgive us our many sins, and give us grace to begin again.

XII.

Tuesday after the Second Sunday in Lent.

THE SINNER HOMELESS.

PSALM CVII. 4.
"They went astray in the wilderness out of the way; and found no city to dwell in."

THE old legend of the Wandering Jew tells us how he who had struck and insulted Jesus as He left the Judgment Hall was condemned to wander homeless through many lands, a stranger, unwelcomed and uncared for, who found no city to dwell in. The legend is not without its teaching. Those who wilfully sin against Jesus and the Truth wander through the wilderness of the world out of the right way. They are in a barren and dry land where no water is—no water of life, no water of grace, no water of penitent tears. They are homeless, they find no city to dwell in. Like the Prodigal, they have left their Father's House, their true home; they have wandered from the true Food, and they are hungry; they have deserted the true Fountain, and they are athirst—" Hungry and thirsty, their soul fainted in them." They have shut themselves out of God's House, and it is no longer home to them. They are possessed by devils of evil lust and passion, and they can no longer live among God's people—their dwelling is among the tombs, with those who are dead in trespasses and sins. As long as they remain in this state they can have no fellowship with God, or those who love God. They have no part or lot with them; they shrink from holy things as a naturally dirty person shrinks from a bath—they do not *want to be clean*.

As long as a man goes on living in wilful sin he tries to get away from God, or from anything that reminds him of God. The presence of God's Priest is hateful to him, because it seems to bring a reproach. He sneers at the Bible, just because he is afraid to hear the truth about himself. He calls Church-going cowardly superstition, just because he is afraid to listen to what the Church says about impenitent sinners. He says to the Priest, to the Bible, to the Church, "Hast thou found me, O mine enemy; hast thou come to call my sin to remembrance?"

For those who prefer the dwelling among the tombs, who would rather be possessed by the devil than filled with the Holy Ghost, there is no hope. But to those who have wandered out of the right way, who are conscious that they have fallen into evil, and who desire to return, I would say—

> "And wilt thou seek again
> Thy howling waste, thy charnel-house and chain,
> And with the demons be,
> Rather than clasp thine own Deliverer's knee?
> Sure 'tis no Heaven-bred awe
> That bids thee from His healing touch withdraw;
> The world and He are struggling in thine heart,
> And in thy reckless mood thou bidd'st thy Lord depart."

Let us not be of those who asked Jesus to depart out of their coasts, but rather let our prayer be, "Abide with us, for it is toward evening." "They cried unto the Lord in their trouble, and He delivered them from their distress !" We all like sheep have gone astray, but the Good Shepherd will hearken to our cry for help. He says to us—

> "O silly sheep, come near Me,
> My sheep should never fear Me,
> I am the Shepherd true."

Never be ashamed to cry unto the Lord ; our safety lies in that. We must not expect to be able to bear our troubles alone and in silence, like the stoical Indian burning to death at the stake without a cry. We must not expect to fight the grim battle of life in our own strength, to keep in the narrow way by our own carefulness, or to trample upon temptation by the sheer force of our own will. We must learn our weakness, we must get to see how easily and how often we go wrong, how frequently we stray from the home of peace into the wilderness, out of the way. There we shall cry out to the Lord in our distress. When we have been brought low, when God in His love has sent trouble upon us, then the proud heart will be humbled, then the locked lips will be unloosed, then the cry will go up, " Lord, be merciful to me, a sinner."

Believe me, God loves to hear His children crying to Him, just as to an earthly father's ear there is no music like the voice of his child. Let our cry go up now, and Jesus will hearken, and will lead us forth by the right way, the way of repentance, which leads to the way of joy and peace, till we reach our own city, the Heavenly Jerusalem, which is above, and is the mother of us all.

Blessed Jesu, we have wandered from the right way, we have followed too much the devices and desires of our own hearts; hear our prayer, and let our cry come unto Thee. Lead us back by the right way, that we may return to Thy Fold, and to our Father's House.

XIII.
Wednesday after the Second Sunday in Lent.

THE GOOD THINGS OF GOD.

PSALM CVII. 8.

"O that men would praise the Lord for His goodness, and declare the wonders that He doeth for the children of men."

THE Bible constantly sets before us the duty and privilege of praising God. The Book of Psalms is especially a teacher of praise. But, as a rule, I think this duty of praise is neglected, if not altogether forgotten. If I were to ask you one by one why you have come to Church to-day, what would your answer be? Would anyone say truly, "I have come to praise the Lord for His goodness, and to declare the wonders that He doeth, has done, will do, for me and all the children of men?"

No; you would say, if you spoke the truth, "I have come to pray to God because I want something; I have come to hear the Bible read, and the sermon preached, because I want to get good. I go to Holy Communion for the same reason."

Now this is mere selfishness. This is merely *getting* all and *giving* nothing. God asks for your praises— "Whoso offereth praise glorifieth Me." What we need to do is to endeavour, as much as possible, to get rid of self, and thinking of self. Self-conscious people are ever the most unhappy, because they are always fancying that they are slighted or misunderstood. In their religion they are specially miserable, because all their devotion is full of self, and self-pleasing, so that there is no room for God. In very many cases we are singing or saying *our own* praises, and declaring our own wants and wishes, instead of uttering the praises of God, and magnifying His Holy Name.

If you recall the hymns which are most popular you will see how true this is. We hear of people frequenting a particular Church because they like the music there— because they *enjoy the Service*—as if the Service were specially for their pleasure. They speak of their favourite hymn, and they sing it because they like it, and refuse to sing another hymn because they dislike the tune.

All this is mere self-worship. Those very hymns which are most popular are all about self. They are supposed to be sung to the praise and glory of God, but as a fact they are full of self, and talking of self. We sing that

> "I could not do without Thee,
> O Saviour of the lost!"

or again,

> "I greatly long to see
> The special place my dearest Lord
> In love prepares for me;"

and so on in many other hymns. This is not praising God, it is thinking of ourselves. We shall never praise Him rightly till we get farther away from self, till the one great desire of our life is to be

> "Nearer, my God, to Thee,
> Nearer to Thee."

It was the sin of Israel of old, and the root of most of their evil doings, that they kept not God's great goodness in remembrance. If we only would dwell upon the good things which the Lord has done for us, and always is doing, our mouth would always be showing forth His praise from one generation to another.

"O that men would praise the Lord for His goodness." What is this goodness, what are the good things of God? How can we reckon them up? Broadly speaking, they are our creation, preservation, and all the blessings of this life; and above all, the redemption of the world, the means of grace, and the hope of glory. What earthly life is long enough wherein to praise and glorify God for such good things as these! We have need to praise God because He has taken us—poor waifs and strays—out of a hard, and selfish, and sinful world, and made us His own children by adoption, and placed us in His own Family, the Holy Church. He has given us a home here in His Church on earth, and He promises to all who obey Him a home eternal in the Heavens. For this we have need to bless and praise God's Holy Name.

Then He has given us the true Faith. Whilst the world outside is fighting and disputing over various forms of belief or unbelief, whilst each teacher would have us accept his special faith, God gives us in the Church *the* Faith once delivered to the Saints, which is held by all true Christians always and everywhere. For this Holy Faith we have need to praise God.

Then we should praise Him for our preservation, both of soul and body. We have wandered out of the right way like lost sheep, and have strayed from home like the Prodigal, yet God has in His mercy brought us back again. The Good Shepherd has sought and found the sheep, the Father has welcomed back the prodigal.

Brethren, ask your own hearts to tell you how good the Lord has been to you. Can you recall no special good thing which He has done for you? Think—that blessing, unexpected, undeserved, that came to you; that grievous sin so tenderly, so freely forgiven; that grace and comfort in the hour of need, that strength sent to help you to bear a heavy weight of affliction—can you remember some of these good things?

Blessed Jesu, open our lips that our mouth may show forth Thy praise. Let our song be always of the lovingkindness of the Lord. Teach us to forget ourselves and to think of Thee. So shall Thy praise be ever in our mouth.

XIV.
Thursday after the Second Sunday in Lent.

THE WONDERFUL THINGS OF GOD.

PSALM CVII. 8.
"The wonders that He doeth for the children of men."

I SPOKE to you of the good things which God has done for us, and for which we should praise Him. Next, we should praise Him for His *wonderful* acts to us and to all men. Think of the Incarnation, of God taking our flesh, and dwelling among us in lowliness and humility, to set us right, to set us free, to undo what Adam's sin had done.

Is there anything so wonderful as the lowly birth at Bethlehem, the gentle boyhood, the patient, laborious manhood of Christ Jesus? But if the Incarnation is wonderful, the Passion, the Suffering, of the Man of Sorrows, is still more so. It was not only the agony of body which Jesus had to bear. Others have suffered persecution, insult, scourging, even as He did. Others have endured the pains of the cross. But no one, except the Son of God, has borne the weight of the sins of the whole world, and this it was which made the sufferings of Jesus greater, more wonderful, than any other.

The wonders that He doeth for the children of men go on in an ever-increasing scale—still more marvellous is the Resurrection. If the work of Jesus had stopped short at Calvary we should have been left of all men most miserable, with nothing but a dead Christ to worship. We should have known that in Adam all men die, but nothing beyond. The Resurrection gave us a hope of immortality which makes us strong to do and dare, and to suffer all things.

There are times when the sorrows of this life press very heavily upon us; we seem to be walking through a vast graveyard; all that we hold dear is buried out of sight, there is no voice of any that answers. Husband, wife, little child, alike are silent—it seems as if death ruled all. Then it is that our faith in the Resurrection comes to our aid. Then we can say, "My buried flower will blossom in the spring-time; I believe in the Resurrection, and the life of the world to come." So with the Ascension of our Lord, and with the coming of the Holy Ghost; they are all wonders, whereof we have need to rejoice.

But besides these things, God has done wonders for each of us—individually. We forget them, I know; we do not come back, like the grateful Samaritan leper, to thank God. As the Dead Sea drinks in the river Jordan, and is never the sweeter; as the ocean drinks in all the other rivers, and is never the fresher; so we too often receive the good things, the wonderful things, of God, and are still ungrateful. I have heard hundreds of people talking of their troubles and misfortunes; I cannot recall half-a-dozen who told of the blessings which God had sent them.

Brethren, has not God done wonders for *you?* Is there no one here who was once dead in trespasses and sins, dead and buried in the grave of some evil habit, some absorbing lust, to whom Jesus came one day and said, "Come forth?" Do you remember, my brother, how you felt the stone rolled away from the sepulchre, how the grave-clothes of your sin were loosed, how you shrank from the old evil life as you would from a foul charnel, how you began a new life in the light of Jesus? Is there one here who had lost faith and hope, to whom the world seemed all dark and unsatisfactory, the past a mournful memory, the future a black uncertainty? Do you recall that dark time when you saw no good in your fellow-men, and so, losing sight of God's image in man, you lost sight of God? And do you remember how the Lord led you back to light, and life, and hope, and the dark cloud rolled away, and your eyes were opened, even as were his at Jericho? Is there one here who once loved this present world too well, whose whole heart and soul were fixed on treasure of the earth, till God in His mercy took away your treasure, broke your idol, led you out of Vanity Fair to Gethsemane and Calvary, and gave you treasure in Heaven, even that peace which the world cannot give? Are there no hearts here, once hard and cold, now warm with the love of God? Are there none once careless and frivolous, now earnest workers for Jesus and His Church?

How have these changes come about? "It is the Lord's doing, and it is marvellous in our eyes." "The right hand of the Lord bringeth mighty things to pass." These are the wonders that He doeth for the children of men.

Surely much of our religious teaching is quite wrong, and represents God in a false light. Much of this teaching pictures God as a cruel taskmaster, always on the look-out to punish us. As it has been well said, instead of preaching "Repent ye, for the Kingdom of *Heaven* is at hand," some of our teachers seem to be saying, "Repent ye, for the Kingdom of *Hell* is at hand." They bid us accept salvation now, at once, and so shall we be safe, as though God were only waiting an opportunity to ruin us for ever. This kind of insurance against God's wrath is utterly contrary to the teaching of the Gospel, which tells us that God desireth not the death of a sinner, but that he should rather turn from his wickedness and live.

We may make people unbelievers by painting God as a cruel taskmaster, but we shall only win souls by shewing Him to be Love. Think, then, of the wonders which He doeth for the children of men.

O Jesu, wonderful in all Thy ways, in Thy love, Thy patience, Thy dealings with men, open our eyes to see the wonderful things of Thy law, and the wonderful miracles of mercy which Thou hast done unto us, and to all men. Amen.

XV.

Friday after the Second Sunday in Lent.

THE FULL AND THE EMPTY.

PSALM CVII. 9.
"He satisfieth the empty soul, and filleth the hungry soul with goodness."

A GOOD appetite is a sign of health, just as an unnatural craving for unwholesome food or stimulant, or an absence of any desire to eat, are proofs of disease, and often of approaching death.

The same holds good with spiritual things. God feeds those who have an appetite for holiness. "To him that hath shall be given." The man with a capacity for using his talent in his Master's service has much entrusted to him. The man who can, so to speak, digest and assimilate spiritual food, shall be fed. As honest, wholesome food has no charm for the man whose appetite is surfeited with indigestible luxuries, who, like the Roman Emperor of of old, is ever seeking some new dish to stimulate his jaded taste—so the man who is full-fed with worldliness, with the lusts of the flesh, the deceitfulness of riches, the dead-sea fruit of pleasure, has no desire, no capacity, no appetite, for righteousness. "He hath filled the hungry with good things, and the rich He hath sent empty away."

It is the man who thinks he is in need of nothing, who is surfeited with the food of the world, who is really *empty*— empty because he has not God. His fulness is emptiness, there is no room for Jesus in the crowded inn of his life. "Because thou sayest, I am rich, and increased with goods, and have need of nothing: and knowest not that thou art wretched, and miserable, and poor, and blind, and naked, I counsel thee to buy of Me gold tried in the fire, that thou mayest be rich; and white raiment, that thou mayest be clothed, and that the shame of thy nakedness do not appear; and anoint thine eyes with eye-salve, that thou mayest see." (Rev. iii. 17, 18.)

A blessing is promised to those who hunger and thirst after righteousness: who have a healthy appetite for holy things. And this is a very different thing from being eager for salvation. We often hear people say, "I want to be saved." What do they mean? Very often it is utter selfishness and cowardice combined. They want to be saved from the *consequences* of their sin. They are like the drunkard who begs the doctor to save his life, that he may return to his strong drink again. These do not say, " I want to be holy, I want to be clean, I want to do God's will;" no, their only wish is to escape from punishment; they want to have their sins and yet share with the righteous. Like Pharaoh, they want to be spared " only this once," to have the plague taken away, but there is no sorrow for sin, no appetite, no hunger for better things.

It is the empty, the hungry, whom God feeds and satisfies. Those who try to empty themselves of *self;* those whose thoughts are turned oftener to God and their fellow-men than to their own wants and wishes; those who try to empty themselves of those luxuries and pleasures on which the world spends so much; those who avoid the spicery and sweetmeats of dissipation that they may enjoy wholesome food; these are the empty whom God fills with good things, such good things as pass man's understanding.

And remember that it is only God Who *can* satisfy. The world and its pleasures can surfeit us, and cloy our appetites, but they cannot satisfy. Look at the life of the old heathen, look at the luxury of ancient Rome, no sight could be more hideous, more pitiful. Men sacrificed a fortune to him who invented a new pleasure, which was exhausted as soon as tried. The writings of the time are full of the unsatisfied longing, without the wholesome appetite for better things. " Ever," says one writer, " there rises from the midst of the fount of pleasures some dash of bitterness." Yes, the bitterness was ever there, the skeleton was ever at the feast, the roses were twined around a skull, they were "without God in the world."

Modern England is in many respects worse than ancient Rome. There the Christians were few and obscure, and obliged to hide in secret places. Here the faith of Christ is nominally that of our country, and yet how many there are amongst us who have so filled themselves with the food of sin that they have no taste for the good things of God; their soul abhors this light food, they are not satisfied, they are the rich who are sent empty away!

They who hunger and thirst after righteousness shall be filled. "Ah, but," you say, "what is it thus to hunger and thirst? My life is so unsatisfactory, 'the good that I would I do not, and the evil that I would not, that I do.' I make good resolutions and I break them. I fight against my besetting sin, but I am often defeated. Every day sees me fall and repent. I try to press forward, but do not seem to get nearer the mark." Ah, dear soul, blessed art thou of the Lord! To be dissatisfied with our spiritual state, to long for a higher, better life, to struggle on, though often weak, often conquered, often cast down; this is to hunger and thirst after righteousness. And those who are thus hungering shall be fed and satisfied. God will give us the bitter food of repentance, that we may be able to receive the sweet food of pardon and of peace.

As the Israelites ate the Paschal feast with bitter herbs, so we must taste the bitterness of repentance before we can approach the Eucharistic Feast of Jesus—the true Paschal Lamb. If we can say with truth, "My soul is athirst, yea, even for the living God," then Jesus will give us drink as out of a river, the never-failing river of His love. May we be like the poor, simple, faithful woman, who on being asked if she understood the mystery of the Blessed Sacrament, or if she really derived benefit from it, answered, "Nay, I cannot understand it, but this I know, I go up to the Altar empty, and I come back full."

Blessed Jesu, Bread of Heaven, feed us now and evermore. Give us day by day our daily bread; feed our souls that we may grow in grace. We come to Thee, sweet Saviour, just because we need thee so. Take us, keep us, feed us, never leave us in life, in death, and in eternity.

XVI.

Saturday after the Second Sunday in Lent.

SITTING IN DARKNESS.

PSALM CVII. 10.
"Such as sit in darkness, and in the shadow of death."

THE Greek hero of old time prayed to the gods, "Slay us in the light." He heeded not death so that it came not in the darkness. There are some in these days who would say, "Let us live on in the dark, no matter for light so long as we may exist."

Have you seen the effect of suddenly admitting the sunshine into a foul, neglected, shut-up room? What a scene of dirt and ugliness is disclosed, what loathsome forms of insect and reptile are seen hiding away in dark corners. They cannot bear the light.

There are men and women who love darkness better than light because their deeds are evil. The false and deceitful cannot bear the light. The worn-out old man or woman of fashion, who tries by every artificial means to hide the traces of time, delights in an artificially-lighted and not very brilliant room. Then they may pass muster. But let the bright light of God's sunshine fall upon them, and you see the tell-tale wrinkles, the sunken cheeks, the marks of Time's handwriting. The actor on the dimly-lighted stage may appear to be the character he represents, the king, the emperor, the man of wealth; but look at him in the full blaze of daylight, and you see the painted face, and the tinsel crown, and you know he is but playing a part.

There are those who sit in darkness and shun the light of God's Word because they are not true, not real, and they cannot stand the light. They neglect the duties of religion, the whisper of conscience, the lamp of revelation, because they know that their lives will not bear scrutiny, will not endure the light. The slave of a besetting sin cannot bear the light, it is as unpleasant to him as it is to the reptile lurking in some dark cave.

One of our greatest masters of romance describes a man murdering his companion, a young girl. When the poor victim tries to draw up the window blind the murderer stops her, saying, "There's light enough for what I've got to do." So it is with the slave of sin, he sits in darkness and the shadow of death; he feels *there is light enough for what he has to do.*

Again, those sit in darkness who are in doubt and unbelief. I do not speak now of those who refuse to believe, who do not *wish* to believe, but of those who are troubled at times with doubts and uncertainties, whose faith grows faint and wavering. Let such people take comfort ; if they *want* to believe, all is well. The holiest and most faithful of God's people have at times encountered this wave of doubt, which seemed to go even over their soul. The more our thoughts are turned towards God and things unseen, the more Satan tries to shake our belief.

It has been said that "we doubt once that we may believe always," and this is true of those whose faith is weak, although their love is strong. As the waning lamp burns all the brighter because it has been trimmed, so in some cases our faith grows all the stronger for having been clouded for a little space.

To those, then, who want to believe, but who are troubled by harassing doubts and "religious difficulties"—as the phrase goes—I would say, have as little as possible to do with these difficulties. Do not look for them, or argue about them. There are mysteries in our faith that our poor feeble eyesight can never penetrate here. Why should we blind ourselves by trying to gaze upon the sun in his noon-day might ? Do not unsettle your minds by reading the works of sceptics—philosophers falsely so called. They may take something very precious away from you, but they have nothing but a stone to give you in return for the Bread of Life of which they would rob you. If you love a person very dearly you would not care to read libels on his character written by an unfriendly hand. Well, the libels on the life and work of Christ can only do you harm. The simple unquestioning faith of the child can trust God, can take Him at His Word, can hold fast to the Cross of Jesus. Ask for that faith, ask to be made as a little child, and leave the "difficulties" alone. Study the pattern shown to us in the life of Jesus. Even the unbeliever cannot deny its perfection. Study that pattern, and try to imitate it, then you will have no time for "difficulties."

Science teaches us that our earth is brightened by the sun because our atmosphere is suited to distribute the light around. If there were no such atmosphere the greater part of the earth would be in gloom and darkness, only those parts being lightened on which the sun's rays fell directly. So it is with spiritual light. We may be "dark amid the blaze of noon," because we have no atmosphere, so to speak, fit to receive and distribute the light. That atmosphere is *faith*, without which the light shines for us in vain.

You know how sun pictures, photographs as we call them, are taken. Well, the light is there ready to form the picture, but the plate must be prepared and made sensitive to the light, or there can be no picture. So for us all there is the light of God, but unless our hearts are prepared, made sensitive to receive it, there can be no result, no picture of holiness, no reflection of the Divine Life in us.

Blessed Jesu, lighten our darkness, send forth Thy light and Thy truth, make us to love the light, and to walk as children of the light; O Thou Light of the world, shine into our hearts, and make them bright with the light of faith, of hope, of charity.

XVII.

Monday after the Third Sunday in Lent.

SELF-LOVERS.

2 TIMOTHY III. 2.
"Lovers of their own selves."

It has been well said by a great preacher of our day (Canon Liddon) that the great difference between ancient and modern Christianity is this: the ancient Christians thought most about God, and the majority of modern Christians think most about themselves. We who live in "the perilous times" which S. Paul foretold, cannot help seeing that love of self is a great power among us. It affects our religious no less than our secular life. The early Christian was satisfied to think and speak of God, He was all in all to him. He was content to sit at the feet of Jesus and worship. The modern Christian thinks and speaks of God with special reference to *himself*, his own special needs and wishes. The greatness, the goodness, the beauty of Jesus and His Gospel, were the themes of the early Christian. He gazed upon them with the eye of faith, and was satisfied. He forgot himself in thinking of God.

I fear too many of us in these days forget God in thinking of ourselves. The first Christians were all for *giving* to God honour, worship, self-sacrifice, all they possessed. The tendency of these days is to *get* all we can from God. Too many of us perform our religious duties in the same spirit that we pay the premium on our life insurance—to get a return, and to feel safe. "I want to be saved," is our cry, not "I want to honour and worship Jesus." The feeling of an ancient Christian was to count Christ all, himself nothing, to reckon the sufferings of this present time a trifle as compared with future glory, to count loss of all, gain for Christ, to consider it the highest privilege to spend and be spent in the Lord's service.

Now the tendency is too often to dwell on what Christ has done for us, to take the benefits which He has bestowed, and to excuse ourselves from doing or giving anything by saying that Jesus has paid the debt, and taken our place, and that all is done and finished. This spirit of selfishness is to be seen in our prayers, in our public worship, in our sermons and our hymns. Have you thought how terribly full of self our private prayers are? Instead of the will of God being put first, and the growth of His Kingdom, the Church, we pray for self—that we may be forgiven, that our souls may be saved, that our bodies may be kept in health and prosperity. We ought to be nearest to God and farthest from self when we are kneeling on our knees, and yet very often the fact is just the opposite.

Look, again, at our public services in Church. The ancient Christians worshipped where they could—in the Roman Catacombs, in caves and holes of the earth; always in danger of their lives; but they felt that they *owed* their lives to that God Who giveth all. We too often go to Church for *our own sakes* instead of for God's sake. We go, as the phrase is, "to get good;" to ask for certain good things in prayer, to be taught by the lessons and sermon.

We go to find comfort and consolation, and we do right.

But these are not the most important reasons for Church-going. These things are what we hope to get from God; but what of *giving?* We owe everything to God, and although it is but little that we can do, we are bound to do our best, and to give the best of our time, our thought, our voice, our money, to the *worship* of God. The less we think about ourselves in the matter the better.

We hear people talking of what they like and dislike in the Church, and often shewing evil tempers because parts of the service do not fit in with their views; all this means really that they are "lovers of their own selves," they are thinking of the Church service as though it were for their comfort and pleasure, instead of being an offering to Almighty God. I believe that the ignorant old cottager who said that the clergyman had made a very beautiful prayer *to her* has imitators among many far more intelligent people.

Again, this self-love leads some persons to neglect reverence in God's House. Reverence for God and His Church are what we owe to His Heavenly Majesty, just as we owe homage and politeness to our earthly Sovereign. When people in Church are irreverent, sitting and lounging when they ought to be kneeling, or in some other way robbing God of the reverent homage due to Him, we know the reason; they are lovers of their own selves more than of God.

Let us try to think, in connection with our Church services, not so much what good shall we get from them, but rather what we must give unto the Lord for all the mercies which He has bestowed upon us.

Our modern hymns, as I have already said, offer a strong

contrast to those of the early Church ; the ancient Christians sang about God, we like to sing about ourselves, and our wants and feelings in relation to God.

The old God-fearing merchants of bygone days used to write at the top of their diary at the beginning of a new year, " Laus Deo "—Praise to God ! Alas ! our diaries, our life stories, are too often full from beginning to end, with the one word oftenest on our lips—" I."

Blessed Jesu, Who has left us a perfect pattern of self-denial and self-forgetfulness, help us to love Thee more and ourselves less, and to be willing to offer ourselves, our souls and bodies, a sacrifice holy, acceptable, unto Thee.

XVIII.
Tuesday after the Third Sunday in Lent.

WEIGHED IN THE BALANCES.

PROVERBS XVI. 11.
"A just weight and balance are the Lord's."

A MAN once declared that he wished he had a window in his breast that all men might see his heart and motives. Do *you* wish that ? Would you like your neighbours to know exactly all the thoughts of your hearts ? Husbands, would you wish your wives to know all your secrets, or wives, would you care to lay bare your innermost hearts to your husbands ? You who are parents, would you be the happier if you could see into your child's inner life ? Your boy, who has gone to school, or out into the world, has his secrets hid from you. You think you have the key to all his thoughts and feelings, but it is not so, and he would not like you to look too deeply into his heart.

But more than that, how many of us would like to look into our own hearts at this moment, to discover the motives which have led us here to-day? It is because we fear to be face to face with *ourselves* that self-examination is so greatly neglected. Well, God looks into our hearts, and weighs our motives in His just and unchanging balance; "To Him all hearts be open, all desires known, and from Him no secrets are hid . . . the Lord pondereth the hearts." Many a sinner spends the time in deceiving himself by saying that he is no worse than others, that many do even as he does. He may deceive others as well as himself, but he cannot deceive God, the just balance shows whether the man's life is genuine, real, true, as the finely-adjusted scale of the jeweller tests the true or the false gem or metal by weight.

Our *daily work* is being weighed in God's balances, and it is a weighing for eternity. God puts His laws, His Gospel, in one balance, and our work in the other; if what we are doing is not quite honest and upright, the scale flies up and shows it; we are weighed in the balances and found wanting. If a servant cheats his master by defrauding him of time or labour, if a workman uses bad material, if people neglect God's House and Service, or offer a mere heartless, formal worship, they have defrauded God, they have given Him short weight.

People make a great mistake about their preparation for

eternity. The common idea is that after having lived a busy life in the world for many years, the time comes when we ought to be serious, to set our mind on preparing for the world to come; we ought to "patch up our soul for Heaven." No idea can be more mistaken than this; no question more misleading than that often asked, "Are you prepared for eternity?" It is the duty of a Christian man to prepare for eternity every day he lives from the earliest to the latest. And how? Not by a morbid expectation of death, not by daily digging his own grave, and murmuring "we must die;" not by looking forward to the eternal hereafter as something very sad and terrible; but just by trying to do his duty daily in the place where God puts him, till the night cometh, when no man can work.

A writer says very wisely that we best prepare ourselves for old age, not by lamenting the fact that one day we shall be feeble and helpless, and unable to work, but by doing an honest day's work whilst we can. And we ought to prepare for eternity in the same manner, "by doing our day's work while it is called to-day." Eternity will bring its duties and its work in good time; meanwhile, if we would be fit for them, let us do the work, and perform the duties which God claims from us here. Thus our *daily work* is a weighing in the balances of God.

Next, *temptations and trials* are weights and scales by which God weighs our hearts. Perhaps you are vexed by a spiteful tongue that speaks cruelly and unjustly; that is a balance in which you are weighed to see whether your heart is right with God, whether you bear your trial meekly, giving back the soft answer, not rendering evil for evil. So every other trial or sorrow is a test, a weighing, to prove whether you are the true gold or the base alloy. People fail sometimes to look on their trials in this way; they say with regret, "I am very much tried," whereas S. James says, "Count it all joy when ye fall into divers temptations."

People say, "Why should God take away my husband, the bread-winner?" The husband asks, why God should remove the wife and mother, so necessary to the children; one marvels that he has such bad health, another that he loses his money. "They tell us," say these people, "that God is love," and I answer, So God is love, and your very trials prove it. It is putting you into the scales and weighing you, to see whether you can give up your own will to God's will.

Then, *prosperity and success* are God's balances. Our health, our prosperity, the children round about our table, are all means by which God weighs us to see if we are thankful, and using our good things in God's service.

Then, every *religious rite and service* are means by which God weighs us. The bells ring out for service, that is God calling us. If we make an idle excuse for neglecting the call, God weighs us and knows the truth. Or if we answer the call and go to Church, but leave our heart at home with our work, God weighs us and we are found wanting. God knows those who come to Church to get, and those who come to give; those who come because they love God, and those who come because they love themselves.

Our *Confirmation* was a weighing time. God knew the false and the true, though to other eyes they all seemed alike, God weighed their hearts. Each time the Blessed

Sacrament of the Altar is offered it is a weighing time. If we begin to make excuse and to go away, God weighs our hearts and knows *why* we go away. God is weighing us every day—what does He find?

And there are yet two more weighings to come. At our death we shall be weighed and placed in our proper waiting place till the Last Judgment. Then will come the final weighing and the eternal sentence—" Well done!" or, " Depart from Me."

A man once saw in a vision an angel of judgment weighing his acts in a balance. The sins of his life weighed down the one scale heavily, then the angel took a crucifix and cast it into the lighter balance, and in an instant the faults and failures of his life were outweighed by the merits of the Crucified Jesus.

Dear Lord, help us: give us a clean heart, O Lord; cast the weight of Thy blessed redemption into the scale; so shall we live and not die.

XIX.

Wednesday after the Third Sunday in Lent.

THE RESPONSIBILITY OF LIFE.

REV. XIV. 13.
" Their works do follow them."

NOTHING that we do or say perishes utterly. Every act and every word of ours produces some result, and is followed by consequences good or evil. This makes the very fact of life a vast responsibility. As every wave which breaks on the shore produces some effect upon the land, so every human act and word affects others. Shakespeare says of the dead Cæsar,

> "The evil that men do lives after them,
> The good is oft interred with their bones."

But in truth the good we have done is no more buried with us than the evil. We may forget what others have wrought, we may refuse them gratitude or reward, but the deed lives— good or bad, it is immortal.

> "Only the actions of the just
> Smell sweet and blossom in the dust,"

but the deeds of the wicked, like some poisonous weed, scatter their deadly seed, and leave behind a fatal crop for others to gather.

None of us can stand alone, and act only for self. Selfish we may be, but our very selfishness affects others for evil. "Every act we do," says a thoughtful writer, "or word we utter, as well as every act we witness, or word we hear, carries with it an influence which extends and gives a colour, not only to the whole of our future life, but makes itself felt upon the whole frame of society."

Of every one who has gone hence, from the great leader of men to the forgotten peasant, it is true that "he being dead yet speaketh;" his influence affects *someone* for right or wrong. Our history to-day is an echo of the history of the past, we reap now what men sowed then.

It has been truly said *(Self-Help)*, "the spirits of men do not die; they still live and walk abroad among us." It was a fine and true thought, uttered by Lord Beaconsfield in the House of Commons on the death of Richard Cobden, that "he was one of those men who, though not present, were still members of that House, who were independent of dissolutions, of the caprices of constituencies, and even of the course of time."

"Man comes and tills the ground, then lies beneath," and we say, foolishly, he is gone, and his work ended. Not so, the ground he has laboured on will bear harvests for which he has toiled. We look on some neglected grave, and fancy the dead man there is forgotten, and of no value. Forgotten of man he may be, but not of God, and his works are bearing their fruit. Whilst, then, the awful thought that all we do and say has an influence, a consequence for others, should make us remember the vast responsibility of life, and teach us to weigh well our words and acts beforehand, the fact that every effort to do good *does* good, and is immortal, should cheer and comfort us.

We may be of those who live and work obscurely, of whom the world knows nothing, and for whom it has no rewards; but we are not forgotten for all that, and we shall have our harvest.

> "There must be those who bear the heat
> And burden, as with weary feet
> They toil along the noontide way,
> Nor rest when comes the fall of day.
> Through dewy morns, through tender eves,
> Love's labour keeps them binding sheaves
> Which no man cares for; One on high
> Will count their earnings by and bye."

Yes, "dwell in the land and be doing good—in due time we shall reap if we faint not." And more than that, others shall reap the fruit of our labours.

> "For we who work, and we who weep,
> Nor weep nor work in vain,
> If other hands our harvest reap,
> And other hearts with joy shall leap
> To garner up our grain.

Our harvests to-day come from the toil of long ago. We gather sheaves in our holy Church to-day, but the seed was sown by the saints and martyrs of old time—"The blood of the martyrs is the seed of the Church." We reap to-day the blessings of peaceful home life, of Christian privileges, of Christian hope, but the seed for this harvest was sown nineteen centuries ago upon the Hill of Calvary.

We reap to-day the golden sheaves of military glory and of conquest, but for the seed we must look where Nelson lies dying on the blood-stained deck, on the furrows of Waterloo, or in the nameless grave of Gordon. If we would trace to its origin any act of gentle love, any sweet word of comfort, any noble deed of self-sacrifice, we must look back to the workshop of Nazareth, to the mount of blessing, to the shadows of Gethsemane, to the Cross of Calvary.

Remember, then, that every act and word of ours bears fruit as surely as the seed sown in the earth, and "Whatsoever a man soweth, that shall he also reap." We make our own future, and that of others, by our present lives.

> "We shape ourselves the joy or fear
> Of which the coming life is made,
> And fill our future atmosphere
> With sunshine or with shade.
> The tissues of the life to be
> We weave with colours all our own,
> And in the vast eternity
> We reap as we have sown."

XX.
Thursday after the Third Sunday in Lent.

THE CONSECRATED LIFE.

> ROM. XIV. 7.
> "None of us liveth to himself."

EVERY Christian has a consecrated life. Be his position ever so high or ever so lowly, his life is the same; it has been dedicated to God's service by the holy water of Baptism. "None of us liveth to himself." God teaches us this great fact by the preaching of the world of nature. The flowers come on the earth, and their text is, "We live not wholly for ourselves." The gorgeous bloom of the topics, and the lowly English daisy, alike have their work in God's world. The flowers make the earth beautiful, they delight the eye, they give forth sweet perfume, they minister food to the bee. The trees are well called by the Psalmist "the trees of the *Lord*," for they do their part in God's great workshop. They purify the air for men and other animals to breathe, they furnish shade from the heat, shelter from the storm, and a home for countless creatures.

So, too, the stream hurrying on to the river, and the bird singing his song, are alike workers for God and not for self. We, as Christ's soldiers and servants, are pledged to dedicate our lives and works to Him, to do whatsoever we do *unto the Lord*.

We are told in God's Holy Word that "our fellowship is with the Father and with His Son Jesus Christ;" that "our life is hid with Christ in God." Surely this means that in all our works and thoughts God must have the first place. It was a beautiful fancy that the angel helped Fra Angelico to paint the lovely cherub faces of his pictures, and we may be sure that all work done in the fear and love of God, however lowly and common-place, is worthy the notice and the help of angels.

Never sigh after some exalted sphere and grand work for God; the poor day labourer who does his work honestly and faithfully, the diligent servant, the conscientious teacher, are doing God's work as truly as the greatest in the land. Our sphere of labour may be lowly, and we may not be able to do even that humble work very well, but if we do our best, "looking unto Jesus," God asks no more.

I have read a legend of a monk who, in ages long gone by, spent his time in painting pictures of saints and martyrs, and "the sweet Christ-face with the crown of thorns." Day by day the monk laboured in his lowly cell, but his art was rude and uncultivated; and his pictures were laughed at by his brethren. The poor artist was filled with sorrow. He longed to show in his pictures of the Saviour the love he felt for Him, but in vain; and so he determined to destroy all his paintings. Suddenly lifting his eyes the monk saw a visitor in his cell, wearing a crown of thorns, and saying with gentle voice, "I scorn no work that is done for love of Me." And the wondering artist saw the pictures on the walls transfigured, and shining with a beauty and a colour which had never appeared on earthly canvas.

"Yes, there is meaning in the strange old story—
Let none dare judge his brother's work or meed;
The pure intent gives to the act its glory,
The noblest purpose makes the grandest deed."

Have you heard of the German sculptor who dedicated his art to Christ? He had won fame and honour by his works, which were chiefly subjects taken from heathen mythology, and his statue of Ariadne is still famous at Frankfort. At length he began to work upon a figure of Christ, and when he had laboured for two years, and the statue seemed finished, he called a little child into his studio, and, pointing to the figure, asked "Who is that?" The child answered that it was a great man. The artist turned away disappointed—he had failed. He began anew, and after years of labour once more called a child to look upon his statue. The little one gazed upon the figure with wondering eyes, then, bursting into tears, she murmured, "Suffer the little children to come unto Me." It was enough, the sculptor had succeeded. He declared that during his years of work he had seen a vision of Christ, and that it was thus that he was enabled to transfer the Divine likeness to the marble.

When Napoleon asked the sculptor to carve for him a statue of Venus, he refused, saying that he who had seen Christ would commit a sacrilege if he used his art in carving a heathen goddess. Henceforth, he said, his art was consecrated. So should it be with our lives and works, be they lofty or lowly. We have seen the Lord Jesus Christ, seen Him by faith, seen Him in His Holy Church, seen Him in His Sacraments. We bear in our bodies the marks of the Lord Jesus, "Whose we are, and Whom we serve." Whatever our work be, whether that of the preacher or the soldier, the politician or the lawyer, the physician or the trader, the labourer, the servant, the artizan, let it be consecrated to God's service, let it be a sacred thing, pure, honest, upright, unselfish, holy, acceptable unto God.

Blessed Jesu, Who didst work in the Nazareth workshop to consecrate labour for the sons of men, help us to dedicate our lives and works to Thy service, and prosper Thou the works of our hands upon us, O prosper Thou our handiwork. Amen.

XXI.
Friday after the Third Sunday in Lent.

JACOB—A TYPE.

GEN. XXVIII. 17.
"How dreadful is this place! This is none other but the House of God, and this is the gate of Heaven."

HAVE you ever waited for a telegram, and watched the operator receiving the message? If so, you have known the feeling of anxiety and uncertainty as to what the words would be, and you felt how ignorant and helpless you were to read the message which was so clear and plain to the eyes of the skilled receiver.

Well, the Old Testament is to many people what a telegram is to the uninitiated; it brings an important message, good news from a far country, a communication from our Father's House, and yet we cannot read it aright! Some have even shrunk from the histories of the Old Testament as being unworthy of God's people. Let us, however, look on those histories as they really are—types and shadows of the Gospel—and all will be changed. The mere story of Jacob as a story might fail to edify us. We might even sympathize rather with the deceived Esau than with the deceiver Jacob.

But let us look on Jacob, as the Church always has done, as a type of Jesus, and consider the Patriarch's life as a foreshadowing of the Incarnation, and we shall find gems of precious teaching in every part of the story.

In Rebekah and Isaac praying for a son after long waiting, we see a shadow of God's people praying for the desire of all nations, that long-expected Messiah. In Jacob, driven from his father's house, and becoming a wanderer and an exile because of his brother's hatred, we see a picture of Jesus leaving His Heavenly Father's home, and wandering in the wilderness of this world, and hated by His brethren.

But neither Jacob nor Jesus was alone. Jacob lying on his stony pillow at Bethel is surrounded by holy angels, and over and over again in his exile angels are "about his path, and about his bed." So Jesus, lying despised and uncared for by the world in the Bethlehem manger has a choir of angels to herald His birth.

Jesus, tempted and fasting in the stony wilderness, is ministered to by angelic hands. Jesus, bowed down by sorrow in Gethsemane, has an angel sent to strengthen Him. Jesus, pursued by His brethren and put to death, has angels to announce His resurrection, and to declare His coming again.

Jacob, though a wanderer from his father's house, had yet a vision of Heaven; and Jesus, though a stranger and a sojourner on earth, was in His two natures of God and Man closely connected with Heaven, a ladder, as it were, set up from earth to Heaven.

Look again at the story of Jacob, and we see him suffering hardship, ingratitude, deceit, for the sake of Rachel, whom he loved, and, to gain her, becoming a shepherd, a pilgrim, a servant. Now the name Rachel means a sheep, and we cannot help seeing in Jacob's story a type of Jesus, Who took upon Him the form of a servant, and was called the Good Shepherd, and was despised and rejected, that He might seek and save His sheep that were lost.

For many years Jacob served Laban, and bore his treachery that he might win his bride. And in like manner Jesus laboured among men for three and thirty years, and allowed Himself to be called the carpenter's Son, and bore the mockery of those whom He served, and endured the treachery of Judas, the familiar friend, that He might purchase to Himself a Universal Church, even a Holy Bride, without spot, or wrinkle, or any such thing.

In Jacob wrestling with the angel we see a type of Gethsemane, and the awful struggle between the Divine will and the human will. Jacob bore the marks of his struggle, as he halted upon his thigh; Jesus conquered by giving up His will to His Father's will, and by becoming obedient unto the death of the Cross, and He ever bears the mark of *His* struggle and His victory, even the wounds in His Hands, and Feet, and Side.

One thought more; Jacob is a type of Christ's people as well as of their Master. Jacob was an exile from his father's house for the fault of others as well as for his own. And in his wanderings he had a vision of Heaven. We are all exiles, far from our Heavenly home, because of our own sins and the sin of Adam. But we have glimpses of Heaven vouchsafed to us. There is Bethel—the House of God, the Holy Church, for us. There, in the highest and most Heavenly of all services, the Holy Eucharist, we can see Heaven opened, we can take part with angels and archangels and all the company of Heaven in the worship of God.

We on earth are joined to the Church in Heaven by the Incarnation of Jesus Christ. There, at the blessed Altar, we find the ladder set up from earth to Heaven. And how ought we to draw near? Surely with the thought of Jacob, " How dreadful is this place! This is none other but the House of God, and this is the gate of Heaven." Yes, the place is *dreadful* in the sense of filling us with awe, and dread, and reverence for God present there. But not dreadful in the sense of frightening us away. If you were to visit the court of your Sovereign, you would feel naturally a certain amount of awe and reverence, but if you loved your Queen, and knew that you were well-known and welcome at her court, there would be no shrinking back or slavish fear.

Brethren, we know how Jesus loves us, we know that our names are all known to Him, written on His Heart, as were the names of Israel on the High Priest's breastplate. Shall we hesitate to draw near the Presence Chamber of our King when He says, " Come unto Me, and I will give you rest?"

Blessed Jesu, give us, strangers and pilgrims here on earth

a Heavenly mind, so that we may in heart and mind with Thee continually dwell. Fill us with holy awe and love for Thy Altar, the place where Thine honour dwelleth, and open our eyes that we may see Thee in Thy Blessed Sacrament and be satisfied. Amen.

XXII.

Saturday after the Third Sunday in Lent.

PHARAOH—A WARNING.

EXODUS X. 17.
"Forgive, I pray thee, my sin only this once."

PHARAOH, King of Egypt, is a warning to us against false repentance. When one plague after another came upon his country, when the land was defiled with blood, the houses filled with frogs, and lice, and flies, the crops blasted, the cattle stricken, the country wrapped in thick darkness, and the first-born smitten—then Pharaoh turned to God, and cried for pardon, and promised amendment. But no sooner was the plague removed than the king returned to his former evil way. "When Pharaoh saw that the rain and the hail and the thunder were ceased, he sinned yet more, and hardened his heart."

This miserable Egyptian king is a type of many people now-a-days, who live without God in the world, neglecting His will, and setting His holy laws at defiance, and when sudden misfortune comes upon them turn to God and to religion, just as they turn to the doctor and his medicine. Such people forget God and His commandments as long as they are in prosperity. They take no heed of the Hand which keeps them in safety day by day, and gives them bread to eat, and preservation, and all the blessings of this life. But when the plague of trouble comes, when their property is swept away, or their crops injured, or the pestilence comes among them, and the children are smitten, or death stares them in the face, then they cry unto the Lord, and it is the coward cry of Pharaoh, " Forgive me, I pray thee, my sin only this once!" They ask God to take the plague away from them, and promise to amend their lives for the future. But what happens? God in His mercy sends them relief, the sun once more shines out after the darkness, the sick person recovers, the impending danger is turned aside, and straightway the vows, and promises, and professions are all forgotten, the Bible is put back to the neglected cupboard with the now useless medicine bottles, God is once more shut out of the house, so to speak, and the last state of these people is worse than the first.

A writer of the last century tells us how a woman was crossing the Channel from France to England, and was overtaken by a storm. She was carrying with her some smuggled lace, and when the storm arose and the waves beat into the vessel she fell heartily to her prayers, and thought wholly of her soul; but when the storm abated, her thought and care were entirely for the smuggled lace. How many there are amongst us who only turn to the duties of religion in the hour of peril, and waste all the rest of their life upon some miserable piece of this world's frippery!

Again, there are those who, like Pharaoh, want to make a bargain with God, and so have their own way and do God's will as well. The Egyptian, in one of his moments of fear, agreed to let Israel go, but they were to leave their families and their property behind.

So there are people who in the hour of danger are ready to do God's will up to a certain point; like the young ruler, they are willing to follow Jesus, but they refuse the conditions—to give up what pleases them best. All such repentance as this is false and worthless. True repentance springs from sorrow for sin, sorrow for having offended against the all-loving God. But the repentance of Pharaoh and the many who imitate him springs from a selfish, cowardly wish to escape punishment. This false repentance comes from a wrong idea of what religion is, and of what Jesus Christ came to do for us.

It has been well shown by a bishop of our day that the popular and false notion is that Jesus Christ came to save people from Hell, whereas, He came to save people from *their sins*, which is quite another matter. The bishop says very plainly that the common notion is that there are two places in the next world, one called Heaven and the other Hell. There are people who have no great affection for Heaven, but they have a very great fear of Hell. They never think of living a Heavenly, that is, a holy, life here, and so preparing for Heaven hereafter; but they say that Jesus Christ came into the world to make it easy for them to go to Heaven when they die, and avoid going to Hell. All they have to do is to go to Jesus some day when they are ill, and like to die, and can do no more work, or selfish business, in the world, and tell Him that they are sorry for their sins, *for having forgotten Him all through their lives*, and then He will in some way or other put them into Heaven.

Now such teaching is utterly false. Jesus came to give us strength to get the better of our sins, and to live a godly, righteous, and sober life. If we never look to Him for help all through our days till the last moments come, and then cry out in our fear, "Forgive me, only this once, and let me go to Heaven," it would be unjust, even immoral, if our prayer were granted. We make our own future here, and in the world to come. "Sin makes a Hell wherever it is, and righteousness makes a Heaven."

Blessed Lord Jesu, Who camest to destroy the works of the devil, and to make us heirs of everlasting life, grant us grace to live so near to Thee every day in the path of duty, truly repenting of our daily faults, and striving to do better, daily mortifying our evil and corrupt affections, and daily proceeding in all virtue and godliness of living, that we may begin the Heavenly life here, which shall be ours for ever hereafter.

XXIII.

Monday after the Fourth Sunday in Lent.

S. PETER—A WARNING TO THE IMPULSIVE.

S. LUKE XXII. 62.
"Peter went out, and wept bitterly."

THE fall of S. Peter is a warning against what may be called impulsive religion. Acting on impulse under any circumstances is a dangerous thing, it is specially so in religion. People of an impulsive temperament are usually very lovable, as was S. Peter; they are warm-hearted, generous, sympathetic, quick to feel and suffer, but, like the Apostle, they are liable to great faults. They are often unstable, "Everything by turns and nothing long;" they are apt to act and speak without thought and judgment; their courage is often mere rashness, which may end in sheer cowardice. They frequently lack *staying power* and principle, and the promise of good, "the early dew of the morning," quickly vanishes away. People of impulsive nature are often given to trust in themselves, to over-rate their powers, and so they fall, like S. Peter.

There is a great tendency in the present day to foster a kind of impulsive, or even hysterical religion, and it is specially a danger for those of a warm, generous, hasty, temperament. It is the fashion with certain religionists to force people, as it were, into exotic Christians, without giving them time to *grow in grace*, and as a natural consequence, they develope quickly, like Jonah's gourd, but just as quickly wither away. They appear to come to maturity very fast, like the seed on the rock, but they have no depth of earth, and therefore no root, and so they perish under the hot sun of trial, and the scorching fire of persecution.

There is a great want of *root*, of *depth*, in the religion of too many people of our day. We see them one day running to Jesus, but in a little while they have forsaken Him and fled. Like Demas, they cast in their lot with the Church of Christ, and presently, because they have not counted the cost, they have returned to the world which they loved too well. Like S. Peter, they are ready with the impulsive word, or the quick blow, for Christ's sake, but they cannot watch with Him in the Gethsemane of trial, they cannot endure the cross of persecution or insult for His sake, they lack the moral courage to speak out in the presence of Christ's enemies; they follow Jesus still, but it is afar off.

To all people of this impulsive character I would say a few words of warning. First, do not mistake feelings and emotions for true religion. This hysterical devotion is like an ague fit, hot and cold by turns. S. Peter doubtless *felt* quite certain of himself and his religious faith when he said, " Though I should die with Thee, yet will I not deny Thee." Yet how soon he found himself frightened by a serving-maid into denying his Master thrice ! None of us knows his own weakness, therefore, instead of joining the boastful who talk of being saved, let us ever remember the warning, " Let him that thinketh he standeth take heed lest he fall."

Again, let the example of S. Peter warn us against exposing ourselves unnecessarily to the danger of temptation. The Apostle was so confident in himself, so sure of his courage, and his devotion to his Master, that he mingled with the enemies of Christ. And what happened? S. Peter fell before the very first temptation. To be a friend of Jesus in that company meant danger, and so, when the question was asked, S. Peter answered, "I know not the Man."

Now there is a similar danger for us. We cannot always help meeting with the foes of Christ, but we *can* help thrusting ourselves willingly into their society. We can abstain from the company of those who argue against revealed truth, who sneer at things holy, who criticise Church teaching in a hostile spirit. Many a time the good done by a service in Church, and the lesson of the sermon, has been undone by the talk indulged in at some social gathering directly after, where some of the foes of Christ were met together. None of us, perhaps, would really like such society or such talk, but some would be too timid to speak out on the Lord's side, and so their very silence is a denial of their Master.

Remember, then, that we are all very weak, and mostly great moral cowards, and let us carefully avoid any society, or amusement, or reading, or work which may lead us either directly or indirectly to deny Christ.

Next, let S. Peter's example warn us against sudden spasmodic fits of devotion, which last only for a short time. It is "he that endureth to *the end* who shall be saved." The race of holiness is not to the swift, but we are told to run with *patience* the race set before us.

Sometimes, on the occasion of a Confirmation, or a

Mission, we see people very enthusiastic, full of good resolutions for the future. Let such people be very careful not to let the fire of enthusiasm die down into the dead ashes of indifference. Let them guard against trusting in themselves. Let them, like little children learning to walk, keep tight hold of their Father's Hand. Let them make constant use of prayer and the Sacraments, and other means of grace, that they may go not in their own strength, but by the grace of God, lest they fall like S. Peter, and are compelled, when they think thereon, to weep bitterly.

Blessed Jesu, grant us grace to follow Thee closely under all circumstances. Give us perseverance to go on to the end, and grant that we may not, for any temptations of the world, or any pain of death, fall from Thee.

XXIV.
Tuesday after the Fourth Sunday in Lent.

PALMS AND CROSSES.

S. MATT. XXI. 9.
" And the multitudes that went before, and that followed, cried, saying, Hosanna to the Son of David."

S. MATT. XXVII. 22.
" They all say unto him, Let Him be crucified."

" NOTHING succeeds like success!" When the Lord Jesus seemed to the multitude to be coming to an earthly kingdom, on that Palm Sunday long ago, they had palms for Him, and their cry was Hosanna. When, in a little while, the crowd discovered that Christ's Kingdom was not of this world, and that the Lord was unsuccessful and unpopular in the eyes of the rulers, the cry was, "Away with Him—let Him be crucified." It is ever the way of the world to give palms to the successful, crosses of neglect and of suffering to those who seem to have failed. In the great race of life no one looks at any but the winners.

> "Prosperity
> Is warranty of wisdom with the world,
> Failure is foolishness."

In all ages the world has worshipped the successful, not the good. Let a man climb to the top of the tree, no matter by what means, and the crowd will wave its palm branches, and shout "Hosanna!" in his honour. Let a man fail, let him fall down in the race of life, and the crowd sweeps in and thrusts him aside, or tramples him under foot. Yes, in the eyes of the world success is the greatest virtue, failure the worst of crimes.

It has been said that if Sejanus had succeeded in his plots against the hoary tyrant Tiberius, Rome would have greeted him as Emperor and Augustus. He failed, and Rome hurried him to his death. Cardinal Wolsey in his day of success was as a king among men; he failed, and was at once "left naked to his enemies." When, as a young man, Nelson returned from unsuccessfully chasing the French fleet, men said he ought to be impeached. When his success was secured, every mouth was full of his praises. Such is the way of the world, but it is not a good way, nor a true way, neither is it God's way, nor the way of God's people. The world cries "woe to the conquered," but some of the greatest victories are won by those who seem beaten in the eyes of men, those who are

> "the weary, the broken in heart,
> Who strove and who failed, acting bravely a silent and desperate part;
> Whose youth bore no flower on its branches, whose hopes burned in ashes away;
> From whose hands slipped the prize they had grasped at; who stood at the dying of day
> With the work of their life all around them, unpitied, unheeded, alone;
> With death sweeping down on their failure, and all but their faith overthrown."

These are the men and women who have tried to do their duty in silence and obscurity, for whom the world cares nothing, because their names are not among the successful; they have been defeated in the battle of life, they have fallen in the race, but in God's eyes they are not failures, nor conquered. To such the message comes—

> "They only the victory win
> Who have fought the good fight, and have vanquished the demon that tempts them within;
> Who have held to their faith unseduced by the prize that the world holds on high;
> Who have dared for a high cause to suffer, resist, fight—if need be, to die."

My brother, the world may have no palms, no hosannas, for you; it may be your lot to bear a daily cross in silence, to kiss the rod of suffering, unknown and uncared for. What then? God knows His own; you may be unknown yet well known, and that rod of suffering shall one day be a palm of victory which fadeth not away. The world worships success, not so the host of Heaven. Angels ministered to Jesus in the desert of temptation, in the Garden of Agony;

so God and His angels are nearest to us, not in the day of our glory and success, but in the bitter agony of some Gethsemane, in the dark hour of some fierce temptation.

Who were the real conquerors—Herod and Herodias in in their guilty love, or John the Baptist bowing his head before the executioner? Who were the real conquerors—the Roman Emperor, sitting with cold, cruel face, in the amphitheatre, or the martyrs of Christ lying mangled by the wild beasts below? Who were the real conquerors—Xerxes and his victorious Persians, or Leonidas and his faithful Spartans, who died each man at his post in the pass of Thermopylæ? Who was the conqueror—Pilate in his pride and power, or Jesus dying upon the Cross of shame?

Brethren, which shall we choose, the palms of worldly success, the shouts of worldly praise, or the thorny crown of duty, and the cross which God sends us? When Prussia seemed utterly crushed under the foot of Napoleon after the battle of Jena, the Prussian women poured their jewels into the State Treasury to help their country in the war. In return they received a simple cross of iron. Yet their plain iron cross is held now as one of the dearest heirlooms in many a noble family. So the day will come when we shall learn to look upon what we have sacrificed for Christ as nothing worth, and to find our greatest treasure in that cross, when we are crucified with Christ, that we may be glorified together.

Blessed Jesu, grant us in all things not to seek the praise of man, but of God. Let our aim be not worldly honour nor success, but to do the will of God, and to follow the steps of Thy most holy life. Amen.

XXV.
Wednesday after the Fourth Sunday in Lent.

THE RELIGION OF HOME.

1 TIM. V. 4.
"Let them learn first to show piety at home."

It will not be out of place, I think, to give some of our Lenten thoughts to the religion and duties of home life. The love of home is an instinct planted in the hearts of men and the lower animals alike. We English are specially credited with this home sickness, and even in these days of rapid locomotion we carry with us our home love, our home tastes. We change our sky, but not our mind, and most of us might truly say—

> "Green fields of England, wheresoe'er
> Across the watery waste we fare,
> Your image in our hearts we bear,
> Green fields of England, everywhere."

Homelessness has ever been reckoned one of the greatest of sorrows. A great writer and statesman, who has left us, describes a certain duke who had many residences, but, to his great misfortune, had no home. Philip of Macedon, conqueror though he was, could not restrain his own temper, and after endless quarrels with his wife and son, went away— homeless.

But the love of home merely as home is only an instinct.

The rabbit regards his burrow with affection, the burglar seeks the den where he hides, and loves it as home. But surely to Christian men and women home should mean something higher and holier than this. It is the Christian household, sanctified with religion, decorated with the beauty of holiness, in which the true blessedness of home is centred.

Home without God is no home. Even the heathen Roman had his Lares and Penates—his household gods—which he worshipped beside his hearth. In Christian England to-day how many homes are there where the only household god is the hideous, many-sided idol—Self! In the house where the members of the family are bound together by the bond of common union, communion with God and with each other, where husband and wife, parents and children, guests and servants, are united by the same golden chain of love for God and for their neighbour, in such a place the name *home* is real indeed. The odour of holiness fills the rooms, as the scent of Mary's precious ointment filled the house of old.

In the awful days of the Plague of London an infected house had a great red cross marked on its door, to show that there were foulness and death there. God sets His mark—His Cross—on the threshold of every godly home, as a sign, not of death, but of life, not of foulness, but of sweetness; the scarlet line, token of salvation, is tied to the windows, the Blood is sprinkled on the lintel and the door-posts. Is it so with your home? Ask yourselves that question to-day. You are here in Church, you are observing Lent, at least your presence here would lead one to suppose so; but what of your inner life, the life of the family, have you learnt to show piety *at home?*

I have heard of a man who repulsed a visitor with the words, "We don't want God in this house." Such plain speaking is probably rare, but is it not a fact that there are homes all around us where God is not welcomed as a guest? I am not thinking now of homes where people are living in open sin, nor of the household of the avowed unbeliever; I am thinking of people who are perfectly respectable in the world's eyes, who have a Bible and Prayer Book on their book-shelves, who come to Church perhaps, and yet, if they spoke the truth, these people would say, "We do not want God in this house." Practically, they want to shut up God in His Church, and to shut Him out of their home. They have some vague idea that they visit God in His own House—the Church, but He is not their intimate Friend, their best-beloved Counsellor, and so they do not desire His Presence in the home circle.

All religion is hollow and worthless unless it has love in it. We like to speak of those we love, to think of them, to draw near to them, to fulfil their wishes; but if God's Name is never mentioned in our home, if we dread to speak of Him, as some people dread to speak of a dead friend; if all religious thoughts and duties are locked out of sight, as some people hide away the relics of the dead, how dwelleth the love of God in us? But, you say, I go to Church; is not that enough? And I answer, Some of you go to Church just as you pay a ceremonious call on some person for whom you do not care, and you are glad when it is over. You never tire of going to the house of those yo love; the visit to those you do *not* love is a penance.

Never think that our duty towards God is performed by a grudging attendance at Church. We must not lead one kind of life in Church, and another at home; religion to be worth anything must be always with us, sanctifying, sweetening, brightening every part of our life. Our Lord Jesus Christ by His example sanctified home; His Gospel teaches the religion of the hearth. Christianity is not like a court suit, to be worn on rare occasions, it is the clothing of everyday life.

There is a homely proverb—*Look at home.* Let us do so, one and all. Is Jesus a welcome guest there, or is our home like the Bethlehem inn, where there was no room for Christ?

The followers of Jesus were first called Christians at Antioch. Why? Not only because they held certain doctrines, not only because they worshipped in a certain manner, but because in their daily lives they were Christ-like, men "took knowledge of them that they had been with Jesus." Let us ask Jesus home to our houses, let us pray Him to abide with us, for it is towards evening, and for all of us the day is far spent. And more than this, let us prepare ourselves to welcome such a guest. Let us take heed of our *temper*, to check the angry, pettish, fretful word. Let us amend the idle, frivolous, silly, meaningless talk. Let us fight against the all-absorbing idol of selfishness. So shall our home be happy, "sweet home" in very truth; so shall we be Christians in something more than name; so shall Jesus be our true Emanuel— *God with us.*

Blessed Jesu, come to our home and sanctify it by Thy pure Presence. Hallow our work, our words, our pleasures. Abide with us now and evermore. O come to our hearts, Lord Jesu; there is room in our hearts for Thee.

XXVI.
Thursday after the Fourth Sunday in Lent.

THE RELIGION OF TRIFLES.

S. LUKE XVI. 10.
"He that is faithful in that which is least is faithful also in much."

RELIGION has as much to do with the small things of life as with the great. As the regulator of a watch influences the whole of the mechanism down to the tiniest wheel, so our duty to God and our neighbour should affect our whole household, down to the smallest detail.

No wise person neglects the little destructive moth in his cupboard, or the leak in his roof, or the first germ of disease, just because these things are small. So no one who desires to do his duty as a Christian will regard any trifle as too insignificant to belong to his religion. That religion is essentially one of everyday life. It is not a religion merely of lonely contemplation, a religion only for the desert or the cell; it penetrates not only into the grand Cathedral, but to the homely fireside. It is the rule of life for the highest and the lowest position. It should teach a prince how to rule his kingdom, and a servant how to cook a meal. Camp and kitchen, palace and parlour, merchant's office and children's nursery, minister's cabinet and mechanic's workshop, should alike be managed on the same principles—the teaching of the Gospel of Jesus Christ.

Let us think of some of the small duties of life—trifles I dare not call them, though the world does so. There is our *manner* towards other people. Some of us say that manner is of little consequence, they excuse a man's roughness, rudeness, or harsh behaviour by saying, "It is only his manner." But one of old says more truly, "Manner makes the man," and a former bishop of our Church wrote thus "Temper is nine-tenths of Christianity." The religion of Jesus should make us gentle, courteous, pitiful, patient in our treatment of others. A cold, repellent manner blights a sensitive nature as the east wind does an opening bud. A rough, uncourteous manner shows want of consideration for others, and this is sin. Believe me, there is a religion in all these small things.

The behaviour of some people in Church is highly irreverent, and it is excused as being *only manner*. But, just as it is unjustifiable to refuse civility and courtesy to our fellow-men and women, far more so is it to neglect a reverent demeanour towards Almighty God.

We should all cry out against the man who stood in the Queen's presence with his hat on. What shall we say of those who refuse to kneel, to bow the head, or to assume some other posture of reverence in God's Holy Church?

Religion teaches us to show respect to the feelings of others by our *manner*. There is a striking instance of one who showed his reverence, even for the *memory* of another, in this way :—The emperor of Russia was walking one day in the public streets, when a coffin was borne past him on the way to the cemetery. The emperor noticed that no mourners followed, and enquired who the dead man was. "Only a soldier," was the answer. Then the emperor, raising his hat and bowing his head, followed the coffin solemnly to the grave, teaching, by his manner, a lesson of reverence for the memory of a brave man.

Manner and temper are very closely connected. No one has learned the lessons of the Gospel aright who does not keep a constant guard and watch upon his temper. There are people who attend devoutly to the ordinances of religion, whose lives in most respects are blameless, who yet sin from want of self-control. They gather their household together for family prayer, they are regular in their attendance at Church, and yet they make themselves and their family unhappy by a passionate, a morose, or an irritable temper.

A very common form of undisciplined temper is impatience with trifles. Every household has its small worries, and frets, and troubles, caused by the unpunctuality, or carelessness, or want of thought of some of its members.

Let us remember that it is a duty of religion to bear these small evils patiently. They are very *trying*, you tell me; just so, they *are* trials of our faith, of our patience, and blessed are those who endure the temptation, the trial thus laid upon them.

I spoke just now of unpunctuality as a worry of home life. It is no mere trifle, believe me; I look upon punctuality as being distinctly a religious duty. If then we would have others do their duty at the right moment, we must be strictly punctual ourselves. An irregular household is not a religious household. More especially ought we to be punctual in all religious duties, in our private and family devotions, and in our public services in Church. To be careless in these respects is to dishonour Almighty God. You may remember the withering speech of the French king to some courtiers who were late for an appointment—"You *almost* kept me waiting." Earthly monarchs are not often kept waiting, but how frequently we see people who come habitually late to Church, unpunctual in fulfilling a solemn duty to the King of kings.

Blessed Jesu, grant us grace whilst we live here in the day of small things, to be faithful in the little duties of daily life, and to run with patience the race which is set before us.

XXVII.

Friday after the Fourth Sunday in Lent.

THE RELIGION OF THE TONGUE.

S. MATT. XII. 7.

"By thy words thou shalt be justified, and by thy words thou shalt be condemned."

SELF-CONTROL is one of the most important, as it is one of the most difficult, of duties. Truly speaks the epitaph of a soldier in one of our Cathedrals, which, after enumerating the various engagements in which he took part, ends thus—

> "The hardest battle he ever was in
> Was the conquest of self in the battle of sin."

Many a hero of a hundred fights gets woefully beaten day after day in the battle with self. But we are not only bound to control our acts, but also our words. The sins and sorrows of the world are far more attributable to what men say than what they do. There are people who would not do an unkind act who yet say unkind words, and give wounds with their tongue, which are ever the hardest to heal, since, as the French proverb puts it, " A blow of the tongue is worse than the blow of a spear."

This is a subject which comes home to us all, since we all at times " speak unadvisedly with our lips," and say words which we have cause to regret bitterly afterwards. One of the most important and necessary uses of Lent will be the control of our tongue, the humble imitation of Him Who spake as never man spake; Who, when He was reviled, reviled not again, Who, when He was persecuted, opened not His mouth.

It is the fault of quick impulsive natures to speak before they think. Such a practice is as dangerous as that of firing a loaded gun at random—we never know whom we may wound. One of the grandest lessons which we can learn is to keep silence at the right time. William the Silent owed his great success to having this power; it was said of him, even by his enemies, that he was never known to utter an indiscreet or arrogant word. Few of us, I think, could bear to look unmoved on the record of our words spoken in the last twelve months, those words for which we must assuredly render our account one day.

Let us endeavour, by the help of the Holy Spirit, to keep a guard upon our words for the future; the issues of life and death, the future happiness and misery of a brother, frequently depend upon them.

Truly says a wise writer, "The turn of a sentence has decided the fate of many a friendship, and, for aught that we know, the fate of many a kingdom." Was it not a hasty word which caused the death of S. Thomas à Becket, and plunged the king of England into shame and remorse? How many lives have been blighted, homes broken up, and loving hearts estranged by a thoughtless word, or an irritating letter! The fault of committing harsh, cruel words to writing is a very grievous one. "The written letter remains," says the proverb, and although the writer may have forgotten what he wrote the words testify against him. The Spaniards say truly that, "A goose quill often hurts more than a lion's claw."

Spiteful words, whether written or spoken, are utterly unworthy of Christian men. I know that these words are often thoughtlessly spoken, but a thoughtless blow hurts as much as a premeditated one. We have no right to speak without thought, remembering the vast amount of good or harm which may be caused by a word.

Let us take good heed how we speak disparagingly, or contemptuously, of others, or how we attribute unworthy motives to them. Let us remember who it was who said " Doth Job serve God for nought?" and that we are doing the devil's work when we declare that no one does good except for what he can get.

Jealousy, again, is a fruitful cause of ungenerous speaking. It is a more common sin than is generally supposed. The very best of people are tempted to be jealous of another's success. Ordinary society is strongly tainted with this sad vice, which truly " makes the meat it feeds on." Many a one is rendered miserable, and utters bitter speeches, because some Mordecai has not bowed the head before him, or because someone present is better dressed, or more highly connected, or more noticed than himself. I know nothing more pitiful than to listen to the speech of a jealous man or woman.

Then again, there is the frivolous, idle talk too common amongst our younger brethren of both sexes. I am not thinking now of innocent fun and amusement; those are as necessary to us, and as much God's gifts, as the sunshine. I mean the empty, silly talk indulged in for the mere sake of talking, and which is distinctly wrong, first, as being a waste of time, and next, as being almost certain to drift into something worse. Remember the words of the great philosopher of old, " Be silent, or say something better than silence."

Of grosser sins of the tongue I would not speak now, nor of the misuse of the powers of ridicule and sarcasm, terrible weapons to the unscrupulous and thoughtless. I would only urge you to remember that the mouth of a Christian man has been consecrated, touched, as it were, with a coal from off God's Altar; that the mouth which sings God's praises, which prays to Him, which receives the Blessed Food of the Eucharist within it, may not, without grievous sin, utter words which are false, or frivolous, cruel, or impure.

Blessed Jesu, grant us grace so to guard our tongue that we may always glorify Thee with our lips as well as in our lives, and ever take heed that we offend not in word.

XXVIII.
Saturday after the Fourth Sunday in Lent.

THE RELIGION OF EVERYDAY LIFE.

1 Cor. x. 31.
"Do all to the glory of God."

It used to be the custom, and perhaps still is, in some old-fashioned Churches, to provide a book-box in the pews. The member of the congregation to whom the box belonged would on Sunday solemnly unlock it, and take out his books of devotion. When the service was over the books were solemnly returned to the box and securely locked in, and there remained for another week.

I greatly fear that the same sort of feeling which induced people to lock up their Bible and Prayer Book from Sunday to Sunday pervades much of our religion now. We hide it away all the week, and keep it for Sundays. This is a fatal error. Our religion should be to us as the breath of our nostrils, without which we cannot live. It should influence every act of our lives, from the least to the greatest—it should sanctify all the business, the pleasure, the conversation, the relationship of everyday life.

One of the common errors of the day is to suppose that religion is incompatible with the business of a working life. Nothing can be more untrue. One of the chief uses of our holy Faith is to teach us how to do our business and to perform our work.

It is just in the hurry and rush of busy life, in the intercourse with our fellow-men, in the place of labour and of money-getting, that we need our religion most. Business *is* business, you say to me. Yes, but if you mean that religion is something different, and has nothing to do with business, I tell you that you are wrong. Just as the services of our Church are not arranged for Sundays only, but for every day, so the teachings of the Gospel, and the lessons of Holy Church, are meant for our guidance during our working hours. We need the restraining, guiding, purifying, sanctifying power of Christ's religion to keep us unspotted in the midst of much that is foul; to help us to restrain our temper under much irritation and annoyance; to help us to be patient with the faults of others, and to resist the temptations which meet us at every turn—temptations to greed and covetousness, leading us to take advantage of another's ignorance or necessity; temptations to make money by unscrupulous means, to hide the truth, or twist it to our purpose. Believe me, if we profess and call ourselves Christian men, we must have Christ with us in our daily work. We need to accept the *whole* Gospel as the rule of our life.

I have read of a Jew, who, on being sworn in a court of justice upon a Bible containing both the Old and New Testaments, declared that *he only kissed his own side of the Book*. Many so-called Christians do the same. They accept just such parts of the Gospel as they like, and ignore the rest. They gladly receive the promises of God's mercy, and pardon, and lovingkindness; they are quite ready to accept all the good things which God gives;

but when it comes to their *own* part, when they are told that it is more blessed to give than to receive, that it is better to forgive than to take vengeance, that it is good for a man to suffer loss rather than be unjust or dishonest, they turn away. These people only kiss their *own side of the book*.

But life is not all work; there must be recreation and amusement. Here again the sanctifying influence of our holy Faith is needed. There is nothing antagonistic between amusement and religion, only we must remember that our recreation must be innocent. A Christian people are just as much bound by rule outside the doors of a Church, as inside; that fatal false doctrine that we must be religious inside a Church, and anything we please out in the world, is far too common. In our hours of relaxation, whether they be spent in social intercourse with our friends, or in some other manner, the sanctifying influence of religion must come in, if we are Christian men and women. None of us is free to indulge in any kind of amusement for which his conscience reproaches him, or which he would be ashamed to take part in before his mother, his wife, or his parish Priest.

Let me say a word as to our reading. To many of us it is the pleasantest form of recreation. I do not say a word against the good influences of fiction, as long as it is pure and honest. A really good novel is as useful in its way as a really good sermon. And I *do* say that we, as Christian people, are no more free to read vicious, unclean, and immoral books, than we are to take poison. The press to-day issues hundreds of books which are not fit for any decent man or any pure woman to read; some of them are mischievous from their open, unblushing vice, others from their utterly frivolous folly. You who are fathers or mothers, if these books come in your way, ask yourselves the question, "Should I like my child to read such words as these?" Then for the sake of your children, as well as for the sake of your own souls, turn from the evil books. We pray to God not to lead us into temptation, but if we read words which arouse bad thoughts, we are wilfully putting ourselves in the way of temptation. Let us so try to live, and speak, and act in *all* things, that men may see at all times Whose we are and Whom we serve. As a goldsmith looks for the mark on a piece of metal, so let men see that we "bear about in our bodies the marks of the Lord Jesus Christ."

"O God, forasmuch as without Thee we are not able to please Thee; mercifully grant that Thy Holy Spirit may in all things direct and rule our hearts, through Jesus Christ our Lord."

XXIX.
Monday after the Fifth Sunday in Lent.

THE COMFORTER.

ECCLES. IV. 1.
"They had no comforter."

THIS week has been known by the Church from ancient times as Passion Week, a name often wrongly given to Holy Week, which commences next Sunday.

This Passion Week gets its title from the Epistle of Sunday, which speaks of our Lord as "Himself the Victim and Himself the Priest," in the Great Sacrifice of the Cross. From this time we begin to set our faces to go up to Jerusalem, and to gaze on the great sight of the Son of God dying for sinful men. From this time, "coming events cast their shadows before," and one shadow, that of the Cross, falls all along our way.

Let us to-day think of our sorrows in connection with the sufferings of Jesus. Pain and sorrow are as old as humanity. It is an immutable law that sin brings sorrow, and the Lord Jesus is revealed to us as the Man of Sorrows, because, though sinless, He was bearing the sins of the whole world.

Before Christ came into the world, and bore our griefs, and shared our sorrow, man felt himself alone in his troubles. Of the world before the coming of Jesus it might be said, "They had no comforter."

Read the writings of the old-world authors, and you will see that an undertone of almost hopeless sadness runs through them. Sorrow they knew, and pain they knew; pale death came and knocked at their doors, and would not be denied. The man of wealth and power knew that he must leave his pleasant home and his fair estates, and that of all his trees none but the mournful Cypress would follow to his grave. The gods were in his eyes as cold and uncaring as their effigies in stone; there was no strong hand stretched out from on high to raise up the weak and fallen— "They had no comforter."

Even in the religion of the Jews there was a want. Look at Solomon in all his wisdom and his glory, and then read the mournful words of Ecclesiastes. He sees sorrow and trouble on every side—" Lo, I returned," he says, "and considered all the oppressions that are done under the sun; and behold the tears of such as were oppressed, and they had no comforter; and on the side of their oppressors there was power, but they had no comforter. Wherefore I praised the dead which are already dead more than the living which are yet alive." Such was the decision of one who had climbed to the very height of power, and magnificence, and pleasure; there was the drop of bitterness ever rising in the sweet cup of joy, the shadow of black care ever present, his verdict upon all things was the same—" Vanity of vanities, all is vanity."

The old Arabian legends say that in the centre of the mystic staff of Solomon was concealed a worm, which was gradually eating it away. Yes, the worm of selfishness, of pride, of fleshly lust, was there, eating out the best of the great king's character, and besides that, the worm of care was feeding on Solomon's heart; he, like those around him, had no comforter.

For us, since that first Christmas Day, sorrow and pain are changed and transfigured. Jesus has borne our griefs, and carried our sorrows, has trodden the thorny paths of trouble, even as ourselves. He has drawn near to us as our Brother, our Fellow-Sufferer, the Man of Sorrows, and we can draw near to Him in our troubles, certain of His sympathy, certain that " He knows our sorrows."

To Israel of old, God was known only as the Great and Mighty One Who inhabiteth eternity. To the Christian God is this and more; He is the Brother born for adversity, Who has stretched out a human hand to clasp ours, Who was in all things tempted as we are, and so we go to Jesus in our grief as One Who felt as we feel, and we cry—

> "Thou our throbbing flesh hast worn,
> Thou our mortal griefs hast borne,
> Thou hast shed the human tear;
> Jesu, Son of Mary, hear."

Sometimes we are tempted to wish that we could see Jesus with our eyes, and touch Him with our hands, like the disciples and the afflicted people of old. Sometimes our faith wavers because we cannot do this, and we almost feel that the Christ of to-day is not the Christ of the Gospel. Yet our Master said truly, "It is expedient for you that I go away. If I go not away the Comforter will not come unto you." It is expedient for us that Jesus went away. Remember how few among the thousands of Israel drew near and touched Jesus when on the earth. Then think how many millions approach in faith, and touch Jesus ascended into Heaven—touch Him in the Blessed Sacrament, in praise, in prayer, in confession. Solomon of old said "they had no comforter." Jesus has said to us, "I will not leave you comfortless."

"O God, the King of Glory, Who hast exalted Thine only Son Jesus Christ with great triumph unto Thy Kingdom in Heaven; we beseech Thee, leave us not comfortless, but send to us Thine Holy Ghost to comfort us, and exalt us to the same place whither our Saviour Christ is gone before, Who liveth and reigneth with Thee and the Holy Ghost, one God, world without end."

XXX.
Tuesday after the Fifth Sunday in Lent.

THE LONELINESS OF SORROW.

> Isaiah LXIII. 3.
> "I have trodden the winepress alone."

ONE of the sharpest stings of sorrow is that we must, for the most part, bear it alone. We may, indeed, have companions in misfortune with whom we may mingle our tears in weeping; yet every man's special grief is his own, and must be borne alone—"The heart knoweth its own bitterness."

Sometimes in our sad hours some kindly friend will try to comfort us, and say, "I know exactly what you feel," but he does not know. None can enter fully into our griefs and troubles except the Lord Jesus, Who Himself trod the winepress of agony alone. From the very beginning of His earthly life Jesus was alone. Among His kinsfolk at Nazareth He was misunderstood and looked upon with suspicion; among the Jews He was regarded as being apart from them, and a teacher of strange doctrines; by His disciples His words were often mistaken, their thoughts were not His thoughts, neither were their ways His ways. Look at Jesus in the Garden of Gethsemane, how utterly alone He is in His agony! The disciples who have accompanied Him are asleep. He is alone, as far as the world is concerned; and yet He is not alone, for His

Father is with Him, and the ministering angel of comfort.

So it is with us. If we are trying to be Christ's disciples we must expect to stand alone, and suffer alone. The man who tries to follow the example of his Saviour Christ, and to be made like unto Him, must stand above the commoner, coarser elements of the world. He must be, though in the world, not of it; he must breathe a purer, higher atmosphere than that of the mere selfish worldling, and this will make him a mark for misunderstanding, for ridicule, perhaps for persecution.

The man who has no real love for God, no high sense of religious duty, cannot enter into the feelings of an earnest Christian, and so he looks upon him as an enthusiast, a fanatic, or perhaps sneers at him as a hypocrite.

As far, then, as the world is concerned, the Christian in the path of duty must expect to be alone. And yet such an one is never alone. Jesus, the solitary Sufferer in Gethsemane—Jesus, the Man of Sorrows, is with His servant, ever whispering the blessed assurance, "My strength is sufficient for thee."

It has been truly said that three cups are offered to each of us—the cup of temptation, the cup of sorrow, and the cup of death. When these come to us we are in Gethsemane, and if we be Christ's people, He is with us, and His holy angels come to succour us. As far as the world is concerned, we must drink of these cups alone. The world will offer its spiced cup of tempting sin, but it will not help us to turn from it. The bitter cup of sorrow, of bereavement, of disappointment, of pain, is placed to our lips, and we must drink of it alone.

> "Why should we faint and fear to live alone,
> Since all alone, as Heaven has will'd, we die.
> Not even the tenderest heart, and next our own,
> Knows half the reasons why we smile and sigh."

Yes, in the time of sorrow we are in Gethsemane, alone with Jesus. Our friends, however loving, cannot enter into the secret feelings of our heart; only He, to Whom all hearts be open, can fully understand.

> "Every pressure of this Thy Cross,
> Every touch of its bitter force;
> All the sorrow, unmarked, unguessed,
> All the tears from the world repressed;
> All the anguish that pleading cried,
> And the heart-sick sense of a prayer denied,
> I know, My chosen, I count, I see;
> Think not thy God hath forgotten thee."

Then comes the last cup—the cup of death. That must be tasted alone. It was the hideous fashion in France, during the seventeenth century, to surround the death-bed with frivolous company. So died Cardinal Mazarin, with gay ladies playing cards by his side. But for all that, he and the rest *died alone*. In thought and feeling the dying were alone, alone with their conscience, alone with their God.

The Christian, however, is never alone, however lonely he may seem to be. In the time of temptation, in the day of sorrow, in the hour of death, the Good Shepherd is with us, His rod and His staff comfort us.

When S. Francis Xavier was dying he was on board a vessel bound for Siam. At his own request he was removed to the shore, that he might die with greater composure. There, stretched on a naked beach, with the icy blasts of a Chinese winter blowing over him and aggravating his pains, the dying Missionary seemed utterly alone. Yet it was a solitude which some of the happiest of men might have envied, for the dying martyr could see beyond the veil, and knew the presence of the bright and holy ministers of mercy waiting to bear his soul to the Paradise of God.

Blessed Jesu, Who for our sake didst tread the winepress of suffering alone, be with us in our times of temptation and of trouble, strengthen us to bear our cross, and in the hour of death, Good Lord, deliver us.

XXXI.

Wednesday after the Fifth Sunday in Lent.

JUDAS AND MATTHIAS—A CONTRAST.

S. LUKE XXII. 48.
"Jesus saith unto him, Judas, betrayest thou the Son of Man with a kiss?"

ACTS I. 26.
"The lot fell upon Matthias."

THERE is a wonderful contrast between the stories of Judas and Matthias. Both had great spiritual advantages, both were followers of Jesus, and had seen His miracles, and listened to His teachings. Yet the one was taken, the other left. The one betrayed His Master, and died impenitent, a traitor and a suicide. The other laboured as a chosen servant of his Lord.

The same story is repeated amongst ourselves. We are baptized into the same Body, we are taught the same truths, we kneel side by side in the same Church, we come to the same Altar, yet some lead holy, self-denying lives like Matthias, others betray Jesus by grievous sin like Judas. So the unbeliever points mockingly at our Church Services and Sacraments, and denies their use, because he can show us a Church-goer or a Communicant whose life is bad. "Where is the use of Baptism?" he asks, and tells us of the baptized child who has grown up to be a thief, or a liar, or unclean. He asks, "Where is the use of Holy Communion?" as he points out those who have been confirmed and become Communicants, who have gone back and fallen into grievous sin. "Where is the use of praying and preaching when there are those who attend to both and yet lead bad lives?"

The fault is not in the Sacraments or the Services, but in the people themselves. The poisoned man cannot take good food, but you do not blame the food. The seed cannot grow on the stony ground, but you do not blame the seed.

Judas is a warning, not so much to the open evil-liver as to those who profess religion. He began well, he believed in Jesus, he forsook all and followed Him. He listened to the words of life spoken by the Lord, he took part in all the holy exercises of the Apostles; he himself was a chosen Apostle, and had the same powers and advantages as the rest. Probably he was a keen, clever man of business, and so to him was entrusted the task of keeping and spending the money of the Apostles. How, then, came it to pass that Judas fell? Because he did not struggle against his besetting sin—love of self and love of money. He did not ask that his religion might sanctify his daily life. He was ready enough to follow Jesus, and to hearken to His teachings, but he wanted to have his own selfish way as well—he did not let the Gospel leaven his life. So the besetting sin grew upon him; he was trying to serve two masters.

In spite of his being near to Jesus, and constantly employed about holy things, Judas became a thief, and finally betrayed his Master for a few pieces of silver! So he who had begun so well ended as a devil.

"Jesus said, Have I not chosen you twelve, and one of you is a devil." Yes, when we sin wantonly against light, and truth, and conscience, we literally sell ourselves to the devil, and he drives us to our ruin as he did Judas.

Judas, an Apostle, one close to Jesus, able to touch Him, to listen to Him daily, yet fell "like Lucifer, never to hope again." Why? Because he wanted to retain his sin as well as his Saviour. How many do the like! They have no objection to religion; they even like its teachings and its services, but they want to keep their sin as well. Such people betray their Master even as Judas did. Like him, they have not counted the cost of being a follower of Christ.

The man who in his working business life is unscrupulous, who does what pays best, not what is right, who takes the way of the world as his standard, and who also comes to Church, and takes holy words upon his lips, perhaps receives the Blessed Sacrament—such an one is trying to serve two masters, God and the world; he wants to keep his sin and yet be saved; he is betraying Jesus with a kiss. The man who professes and calls himself a Christian, who carefully attends to the outward ordinances of the Faith, and yet sins habitually with his tongue, either by angry words, or false words, or unclean words, is betraying Jesus with a kiss. In a word, if our religion is real, not mere hypocrisy, it must be the guide, the rule of *all* we do and say, it must be the leaven which leavens the whole lump of our lives. We may bear the name of Christian, we may come to Church, we may believe that we love God, and yet we may betray our Master as Judas did. He partook of the Blessed Sacrament of the Last Supper, and immediately went forth to plot the death of Jesus. Every time we draw near to the Altar we are reminded of that awful fact by the words, "In the night in which He *was betrayed* He took bread."

Let us not mistake outward observances of religion for the religion itself. Unless we show forth our faith in our lives our faith is vain. It is not those who cry "Lord, Lord," who shall enter Heaven, but they who do the will of our Father in Heaven. Let us examine ourselves, let us see whether our religion be real and honest, or only the cloak of hypocrisy covering a sinful and a careless life. Let the awful example of Judas remind us of the danger of neglecting the beginnings of evil; his greed and selfishness grew unchecked till they ruined him. So there are many now who begin with Jesus, and are occupied with holy things, who by neglecting their besetting sin at last come to betray their Master.

Blessed Jesus, Who wast betrayed into the hands of wicked men for our sake, grant us grace to fight against our sins, so that we may avoid the awful sin of the traitor Judas, and follow the holy example of Matthias.

XXXII.
Thursday after the Fifth Sunday in Lent.

TRUE MANHOOD.

1 TIM. II. 5.
"The Man Christ Jesus."

WE sometimes hear people pleading their manhood as an excuse for their sins. They listen to the teachings of the Church and the Bible, and then try to escape the standard of conduct there set up by saying that it is too high for them. "We are just ordinary men," they say, "not saints, and poor human nature is very weak." Others take refuge in the foolish belief that religion is not manly, and that whilst its observances are good enough for women, men need a different life in a rough world.

If we were heathens, if the Gospel had never been given to us, if the Son of God had never become Man, and taken our flesh, we might talk in this way. The Incarnation of Jesus Christ shows us what a true man should be, it teaches us the dignity of manhood, it proclaims that only the good man, the religious man, is worthy of the name of man. We may be strong working machines, or clever thinking machines, or talking machines, but we are not fit to be called *men* unless we are trying to follow the example of true manhood given us in Jesus Christ, unless we can say with truth, " The life that I live now in the flesh I live by the faith of the Son of God, Who loved me, and gave Himself for me."

You will say, perhaps, that man is so weak, so easily tempted, so liable to fall. Yes, man is by nature a poor creature enough. But every man has two parts—one natural, one supernatural. There is his natural weakness and the all-powerful grace of God.

> " Unless above himself he can
> Erect himself, how poor a thing is man."

I met a man lately in travelling, and remonstrated with him for swearing. And his excuse was that when beaten in an argument he *must* swear! How pitiful, how unmanly a confession, how far removed from S. Paul's words, " I can do *all* things through Christ Who strengtheneth me."

It is a common thing for persons to excuse their faults on the plea that their circumstances are different from those of others. They tell us, if they are impatient in temper, that no one ever had to bear the provocation which comes to them. If they fall into grievous sin they declare that no one was ever so severely tempted. If fretful, or hopeless, or despairing, they tell us that no one ever had to endure such sorrows, such pain, such disappointment.

Now, this is not true. Each of us thinks his own burden the heaviest; but, as a rule, we suffer just what others are suffering, as no temptation, nor sorrow, overtakes us except such as are common to men. But, above all, there remains the fact that One suffered all that temptation, all that sorrow and agony, can bring.

Jesus, "Who would feel all that He might pity all," says to us, "I, too, am a Man." There are times when we look in vain for the sympathy of our fellow-men. They have nothing in common with us, they do not understand us. The well-fed man cannot understand the feelings of the starving, nor the rich man those of the struggling poor. The thick-skinned, slow-witted man, is powerless to enter into the thoughts of his highly-strung, sensitive neighbour. But thanks be to God, Jesus is not only Almighty God, but Perfect Man, Who not only knows all our feelings, our needs, our weaknesses, and can thus perfectly sympathize, but also gives us a model of life, and the means to imitate it. We do not ask help from those whom we feel cannot understand us. The sorrowful go to those who have known sorrow; the bereaved seek those whose house has been left unto them desolate. As men, we might shrink in fear from God so far above us, but we can draw near to Him as Man, "tempted in all things as we ourselves, yet without sin," and can say, "Thou, Lord, knowest whereof I am made."

The godless man may say, "I am a man, and therefore I yield to temptation; flesh is weak, so I give way to the lusts of the flesh." Not so the Christian; he says, "I am a man, and therefore the Man Christ Jesus is my Brother and my Friend. If I am tempted, I can think of the wilderness and Jesus tempted of the devil—and I know that He will help me to resist the tempter. If I want my own way, and wish to set up my own will against the will of

God, I can think of Gethsemane, and see Jesus bowed to the earth in the agony of that struggle between the human will and the Divine. Then I know that my Master has passed this way before me, and I can hear Him say, "I, too, am a Man," and so I learn to say, "Not my will, but Thine be done." If sorrow and loss come upon me, if those dearest are taken away, or if those whom I trusted deceive and disappoint me, I can look on Jesus, homeless and friendless, Jesus weeping for Lazarus, Jesus deserted by His disciples, and betrayed by His familiar friend, and I can feel that my Master has passed *this* way before me. If the burden laid upon me seems heavier than I can bear, I think of Jesus fainting beneath the Cross, and crying in agony, "If it be possible, let this cup pass from Me." I can recall those words of comfort, "He was in all points tempted like as we are."

Here lies the secret of true manhood—to be made one with the Man Christ Jesus, to be made like unto Him. For this end He has given us the Blessed Sacrament of His Body and Blood, that we may thereby be joined unto Him, that our vile bodies may be made clean by His Body, and our souls washed in His most precious Blood, and that we may ever abide in Him, and He in us.

XXXIII.
Friday after the Fifth Sunday in Lent.

CRUCIFIED WITH CHRIST.

> PSALM XXII. 7.
> "All they that see Me laugh Me to scorn."

EVERY word of this Psalm is the cry of a breaking heart. It was written by David in the day of his great trouble, but Jesus has shown most clearly that it was a prophecy of Himself. On the Cross the Saviour uttered the very words with which the Psalm begins—"My God, My God, why hast Thou forsaken Me?" and in every verse of it we can trace the shadow of the Cross of Calvary. "All they that see Me laugh Me to scorn, they shoot out their lips, and shake their heads, saying, He trusted in God that He would deliver Him, let Him deliver Him if He will have Him!" Those mocking words spoken in the days of David were actually repeated by the Jews beneath the Cross of Jesus; thus they condemned themselves out of their own Scriptures.

So is it with the unbelievers of to-day; when they see Jesus as present in His Holy Church, they laugh Him to scorn, they mock at holy mysteries, they call our worship superstition and priestcraft—the scene of Calvary is reproduced over and over again.

The unbeliever of to-day mocks at Absolution, and says in the very words of the Jews again, "Who can forgive sins but God only?" He turns in contempt from the Blessed

Sacrament, and again echoes the question of old, "How can this Man give us His flesh to eat?"

"He trusted in God—let Him deliver Him." So spake they of Jesus; so have they spoken of His persecuted saints. Ah! blind and slow of heart, they knew not that the God in Whom He trusted would deliver His Blessed Son from all His enemies, and make them His footstool.

Those who watched the dying agonies of the martyrs seemed to be the conquerors, but the victory was with those who suffered for Christ's sake. They were delivered out of the bitter pains of eternal death, and could say with their dying breath, "I see Heaven opened."

To-day there are those who point to the Christian, despised and neglected by the world, suffering, starving perhaps, and they ask with a sneer, "Where is now thy God?" But that poor sufferer knows that he is bearing the Cross after his Master; he has Bread to eat which the world knows not of, he is passing through his Calvary, but the Lord will deliver him out of the bondage of corruption into the glorious liberty of the sons of God.

"Thou art He that took Me out of My mother's womb. Thou wast My hope when I hanged yet upon My mother's breast. I have been left unto Thee ever since I was born." One of old says that our Lord might well find comfort on the Cross by remembering that the same Body, now so marred and wounded, was the very same Body which had been glorified with such high honour, which had been conceived of the Holy Ghost, and which, having put on immortality, should be the Blessed Food of His faithful people for all ages.

"I have been left unto Thee ever since I was born." "From the very first," says S. Cyprian, "Jesus was dedicated to the Father and to men. To the Father, that He might do His will: to men, that they might work *their* will upon Him, and reject, scourge, and crucify Him."

In one sense, we, as Christians, may take these words as true of us. We were made God's children by adoption, from our new birth in baptism; at the holy font we were dedicated to God's service, that we should be His faithful soldiers and servants unto our life's end. We are not our own, but bought with a price; we have been left unto God ever since we were born.

"O go not from Me, for trouble is hard at hand, and there is none to help Me." How could the Lord Jesus use these words when all the powers of Heaven and earth were His to command? Because He had chosen, in His great love for men, to suffer alone, to drink the bitter cup of agony, to be obedient unto death, even the death of the Cross. He would not pray to His Father that He should send legions of angels to rescue Him. He commanded S. Peter to put up the defending sword. Of the people, there was none with Him.

We may use these words in another sense. Every day of our lives trouble is hard at hand, the temptations of the world, the flesh, and the devil, assail us, sorrow, and loss, and disappointment, meet us; and sometimes we are tempted to believe that there is none to help us. But in that dark time of trouble let us remember that Jesus felt the same; that He passed through this *loneliness* of sorrow, and that He Who knows our hearts and their bitterness, is with us ready to comfort, " a very present help in trouble."

"Go not far from me, for trouble is hard at hand." That should ever be our prayer—"Go not far from me." We have gone far from God, we have followed too much the devices and desires of our own hearts, but let us pray that God may not forsake us, often as we have forsaken Him. Trouble is hard at hand; trouble caused by our own sin and folly; trouble caused by our rebellious wills; trouble caused by the fraud and malice of the devil. Go not far from me, forsake me not utterly, O Lord God of my salvation.

XXXIV.
Saturday after the Fifth Sunday in Lent.

BY THE CROSS.

S. JOHN XIX. 25.
"By the Cross of Jesus."

A WRITER of the day says, "It is a terrible thing to have outlived Christ, and to have made Bethlehem, Gethsemane and Golgotha historic names or mere spectral shadows."

I fear that this is too true of many of us. The holy seasons of the Church's year come round, leading our thoughts to the Bethlehem manger, or the Garden of Sorrow, or the Cross of Calvary, but we fail to realize the events connected with them; they are to us as spectres of the past, "they come like shadows, so depart." We fail to enter into and understand the story of our Lord's life and sorrow, because we do not dwell sufficiently on it, our hearts are not in the subject. "The world is too much with us," and we are too busy with the work or the pleasure of the moment to watch one hour with Christ in Gethsemane, or to mourn beneath the Cross of Calvary.

And so it is that we fail to see our sins and to repent of them. We are too much engaged, the one with his farm, the other with his merchandise, to heed the call to repentance; but if we would only realize Christ's sufferings, if Golgotha and Gethsemane were real to us, surely we should be sorry for our sins.

We have come now to the very threshold of Holy Week, let us not waste that precious time. It has been called the *Still Week*, let us be still, and know that it is God Who suffered for us, and redeemed us. Let us strive, as far as possible, to be still, and to commune with our own hearts. Let us, as far as we can, turn aside from the busy crowd of everyday business life, and gaze on this great sight. Let us spend as much time as possible in thought and prayer "by the Cross of Jesus." Let us endeavour to go down in true repentance into the grave with Jesus, that we may be buried with Him, so shall He raise us up at the blessed Eastertide, and make all things new for us through the power of His Resurrection.

There were five classes of people connected with our Lord's crucifixion, and there are the same classes now. There was the first group, comprising the holy women and S. John; these were at the foot of the Cross, close to the suffering Jesus. There are such persons amongst us now, who are keeping this holy season rightly, taking their place close to the Cross of Jesus, listening to the dying words of the Saviour, receiving the sprinkling of His Precious Blood.

Then there is the second group, comprising the rest of the Apostles and disciples, who had followed Jesus afar off. They loved Him, but from fear, or want of faith, they would not draw near to the Cross. There are many such now. They love Jesus, but they shrink from the shame and reproach of the Cross, they are tempted, like S. Peter, to deny their Lord, so Holy Week does not find them by the Cross of Jesus.

The third class represents the soldiers who crucified Jesus, unheeding the words of love and pardon which He spoke. Alas, these also are with us, who by their wilful sins crucify the Lord afresh, and put Him to an open shame. By their unbelief they crown the Lord again with thorns; by the wanton sins of the flesh they wound and scar the precious Body of Jesus; by their cruelty and injustice they pierce His Hands and His Feet as with nails; by their hardness of heart and contempt of His Word and commandments they thrust the spear again into the Heart of Jesus. What to these people are Holy Week or Good Friday? Jesus and His sufferings are nothing to them; "let Him be crucified," they say.

Then comes the fourth class, composed of the curious crowd who watched the Crucifixion out of mere curiosity. Those people at Calvary watched the agonies of the Lord, and heard His dying words, but we do not hear that any of them repented, or drew near to worship, or sought to know more of the matter. They beat upon their breasts, and said one to another, "It is a sad sight," and went away.

This class of persons is also represented among us. There are people who read the story of the Passion, who listen to it in Church, and who remain perfectly unmoved. It does not touch their hearts, it does not appeal to their feelings, it seems to be no concern of theirs; they fail to realize *their* part in the Crucifixion. Many of them declare that it is very melancholy to have the subject brought so much before them, and so they gladly go away.

Then there is the last class of persons—those who knew nothing of Christ, or were too indifferent to go to Calvary. These, too, are amongst us now. The heathen of Christian England, who know nothing of Christ, though they live within the sound of Church bells; and those who have heard of the Crucifixion but take no interest in the matter. To these last Good Friday means a holiday, not a *holy-day* by any means; the sufferings of Jesus are nothing to them, and so they stay as far from Calvary and its crosses as possible.

Let us ask our own hearts to which of these classes we belong; how are we going to keep Holy Week—by the Cross of Jesus, close to the wounded side of our dear Lord; or farther off in doubt and timidity; or with the executioners, adding by our wilful sins to the pains of our Lord; or with the curious crowd, coming in numbers to Church, but only out of curiosity, and not with stricken hearts; or with the utterly indifferent, who remain out of all hearing of Calvary?

Blessed Jesus, Who wast lifted up upon the Cross to draw all men unto Thee; draw us nearer to Thee at this holy season, fill our hearts with true sorrow for our sins, and with love to Thee, and grant that we may find pardon at the foot of Thy Cross.

XXXV.
Monday in Holy Week.

THE SEVEN WORDS.—I.

S. LUKE XXIII. 34.
"Father, forgive them, for they know not what they do."

MAY God help us this week to look on the Cross, and away from the world. May He help us to lift up our eyes unto that hill from whence cometh our help—the hill of Calvary. As we stand hushed and silent in the death-chamber, listening with awe to the last words of some dying friend, so let us meditate this week beneath the Cross, and hearken to the dying words of our Best Friend, of Him "Who loved us, and gave Himself for us."

As we have listened to the Sermon on the Mount of Blessing, let us hear now the Sermon on the Mount of Crucifixion. Every word of it will bring reproach to us, for it is the voice of our Brother's Blood, which speaketh better things than that of Abel, and we are verily guilty concerning our Brother. And yet every one of these dying words will carry comfort to us, for they proclaim liberty to the captives, refreshment to the weary, comfort to the sorrowful, pardon to the penitent, life to the dead. What sorrow, what disease, is there for which these seven words are not a cure—medicine to heal our sickness?

If the battle is very fierce, and we are weary even unto death, then we can think of that promise, "To-day shalt thou be with Me in Paradise," and find rest for our soul. If pain and anguish rack and torment us, we find courage and patience in the agonized cry of Jesus, "I thirst."

No other sermon can teach us such lessons as the words from the Cross. They teach us patience in bearing *our* cross, unselfishness in thinking for others, forgiveness of injuries, kindness even for those who despitefully use us.

"Father, forgive them, for they know not what they do." These words were spoken as the cruel nails were being driven through the Hands and Feet of Jesus. Instead of an agonized cry, there comes a soft prayer for those who were torturing Him. Thus in the moment of supreme agony Jesus appears in His character of Mediator between God and man. He pleads for His murderers, for those who sin against Him.

That blessed work of mediation still continues. We sin often, and we need pardon as often as we sin. That pardon comes through the merits and mediation of Jesus. When we draw near to the Altar in Holy Communion we are, as it were, coming to the foot of the Cross. There we plead the Sacrifice of our Redeemer, His broken Body, His Blood poured forth, and Jesus in Heaven pleads for us, saying, "Father, forgive them, for they know not what they do."

Can it be said of us that we know not what we do when we sin? Only in one sense. Not one of us knows the full consequence of any one sin. Just as the man who wilfully poisons a stream of water knows not what innocent people will fall victims to his act, so the sinner who sins deliberately knows not fully what he does. But if the sin of those men who nailed Jesus to the Cross was great, what must *our* sin be, if, knowing Jesus as our Saviour, we yet turn from Him, and willingly become the slaves of those sins for which He died upon the Cross?

Let no one excuse his sin by saying he knows not what he does. The miscreant who blows up a building with dynamite knows not all that will follow, but he does know that he is committing a terrible crime. So we have only to look at Calvary and the Crucified Saviour to see what sin means and what sin does.

Let us, then, gather up the lessons which fall from this first word from the Cross. First, we have an advocate with the Father—Jesus Christ the Righteous! Our weakness, our poor feeble efforts after good, our frequent falls, are understood by Him, and He ever liveth to make intercession, to say, "Father, forgive."

Next, we learn a lesson of *unselfishness*. All our Blessed Lord's words and thoughts were for others. The cruel agony of the Cross could not make Him forget those who had sinned and gone out of the way. He thought first of all of His enemies. We too often think of ourselves, and forget even our friends. Let the perfect unselfishness of the crucified Jesus teach us a better way.

Then we learn a lesson of patience under provocation. We who are so easily provoked, so ready to resent an injury, even a hard word, and to declare that we do well to be angry, have need to look on Jesus praying for those who nailed Him to the tree. How can we, His followers, hope for forgiveness, if we do not forgive freely those who trespass against us? Our unforgivingness closes the way to God's pardon. He forgives only those who forgive. Bethink you of how much you have need to be forgiven. Bethink you how often you have crucified Jesus afresh, and pierced His Hands and Feet by your sin. Then bethink you how He is ever praying for you—" Father, forgive ;" and remember that " if ye do not forgive, neither will your Father which is in Heaven forgive your trespasses."

O blessed Jesu, pray for us. We have pierced Thee by our neglect, our disobedience, our want of faith. Yet Thy property is ever to have mercy, and to forgive; Lord, remember us now in Thy Kingdom, and plead the merits of Thy sacrifice for us sinners.

XXXVI.

Tuesday in Holy Week.

THE SEVEN WORDS.—II.

S. LUKE XXIII. 43.
" To-day shalt thou be with Me in Paradise."

THESE words were spoken to one who was the first to be saved by the power of the Cross. How wonderful that the first-fruits of the Cross should be not a disciple, not a person of rank or importance, but a poor despised robber, an outcast and a felon, one, perhaps, from the bands of marauders who infested the wild country roads, or some common thief from the most degraded quarter of Jerusalem, or perhaps a follower of Barabbas himself. It was to such an one as this that the gracious promise was given, "To-day shalt thou be with Me in Paradise!"

Truly were the words fulfilled that Jesus had come to seek and to save those who were lost, that whomsoever comes to Him He will in no wise cast out, that He is faithful and just to forgive us our sins, and to cleanse us from all unrighteousness. A little while back, and this thief was joining with the rest in mocking and reviling his Saviour. Then even at the eleventh hour, when the pains of death were upon him, he repented, and acknowledged Jesus as his Lord and his God. And so first-fruit of the Cross, the thief passed into the re-opened Paradise which Adam's sin had closed.

Both the thieves offered a petition to Jesus, the one without faith, the other believing. The one said, "If Thou be the Son of God"—even as the tempter said before—"save Thyself and us." The other acknowledged Jesus by his words—"*Lord*, remember me when Thou comest into Thy Kingdom." By the mighty power of faith he was able to recognize in that poor, broken form—stripped, wounded, more marred than any man's—the likeness of the Son of God. The one thief asked for deliverance *from* his cross, the other begged to be saved by the Cross of Jesus—the one desired a temporal blessing, the other the eternal joy of pardon and peace.

My brothers, which do our prayers most resemble? Do we not most often ask for *bodily* blessings, for freedom from pain, or poverty, or trouble? Do we not oftener ask to be delivered from our cross than for strength to bear it patiently? Do we not oftener ask Jesus for worldly prosperity instead of praying for a place in Paradise, a home among the many mansions of the blessed?

Next, let us notice the conditions on which the thief was pardoned—repentance and faith. Both those malefactors were in a like case, and both were equally close to Jesus, Who was dying for their sins, and for the sins of the whole world. Yet to the one came the assurance of Paradise, the other was left to his fate. To the one Jesus spoke the absolving word, to the other He said nothing. Both men were probably equally guilty, but one believed and repented, and was saved; the other died in his sin. The faith of the penitent thief was indeed wonderful. Whether he had ever seen Jesus before we know not, but to acknowledge as his God One Whom he saw hanging like a common criminal, in like condemnation with himself, One Whom he saw actually die by his side before his own agonies were ended, required a marvellous faith indeed.

And how perfectly the dying thief showed his trust, his confidence in Jesus. He does not say "Forget me—forget my dishonoured name, my many crimes." No; his prayer is "*Remember me.*" Surely this gives confidence and encouragement to the greatest sinner, who has truly repented, to draw near to Jesus and to cry, "Lord, remember me in Thy Kingdom."

The penitent thief confessed his sin, asked for pardon, acknowledged his punishment as just, and he received absolution. But he had to bear his cross. Jesus did not promise him deliverance from that. Learn then, brethren, that sin brings its sorrow and its punishment, and even repentance, though it brings pardon, does not give freedom from suffering.

Jesus does not promise us a life without a cross; if we are His followers we *must* go by the road that leads to Calvary. But He gives us strength to bear our cross in the blessed words of pardon, "Be of good cheer, thy sins be forgiven thee;" what sorrow, what trials, can be too heavy for us, what pains of death can alarm us if we have the promise, "Thou shalt be with Me in Paradise?"

In Paradise! Ah, we know not the meaning of that blessed promise. We, whose pleasures are so short-lived, so mixed with anxiety and trouble; we, whose rest is so brief and so quickly broken, cannot picture the perfect joy, the perfect rest, the perfect peace of Paradise.

When the Queen of Sheba saw the glories of Solomon's kingdom she declared that "the half had not been told her." When the weary eyes, which closed in the night of death, open again in the bright morning of Paradise, when the prison-house of this body is once for all open, and we are free, surely we shall have need to cry, "Behold, the half was not told me."

"With Me in Paradise." Ah, surely there lies the true blessedness, the true joy of that new life, it is Paradise because it is *with Jesus*.

Blessed Jesu, Who didst pardon the penitent thief upon the cross, grant us true faith and earnest repentance, so that our sins being forgiven, we may find a place with Thee in Paradise.

XXXVII.

Wednesday in Holy Week.

THE SEVEN WORDS.—III.

S. JOHN XIX. 26, 27.
"Woman, behold thy son . . . behold thy mother."

WHAT a perfect pattern of unselfishness these dying words of Jesus put before us! His first thought was for His enemies, His second thought was for the dying robber, His next for His mother and His beloved Apostle. It was as God, Who alone can forgive sins and open the gates of Heaven to all believers, that He said to the thief, "To-day shalt thou be with Me in Paradise." It is as Man, born of a woman, One Who was the Son of Man by taking flesh in the womb of the Blessed Virgin, and Who knew all the sorrows and pains of humanity, that He now speaks, and indicates S. John as the protector of His mother. Not the long agony of Crucifixion, not the weight of the tremendous burden laid upon Him—the sins of the whole world—could make Jesus forget His mother, in whose arms He had lain in the Bethlehem manger, at whose knees He had learnt the earliest lessons of a gentle and obedient child.

The Blessed Virgin was alone in the world. Joseph was dead, her Divine Son was dying. The sword had pierced through her heart as it had been foretold; Jesus knew her sorrows. As God, to Him her heart was open, and from Him no secrets were hid. As Man, there was the mysterious bond of sympathy and love which exists between mother and child, and so entering perfectly into the Virgin's sorrows, the Lord tenderly provides for her future comfort. He confides His mother to His dearest friend, He gives "a virgin mother to a virgin child." In those words, "Woman, behold thy son . . . behold thy mother," we get a proof of the perfect *Manhood* of Jesus. When He grants pardon to the thief, when He rises triumphant from the grave, when He breathes on His Apostles and says, " Receive ye the Holy Ghost," we see the Hand of God. But in that loving forethought and care for His mother and His friend we see *the Man* Christ Jesus, bone of our bone, and flesh of our flesh, the Brother born for adversity.

Again, those words of Jesus consecrate home life, and teach the sacred relationship between parents and children. There are those who would have us believe that religion means seclusion from the world, solitary, austere asceticism. But such is not the teaching of Jesus. As the child and youth at Nazareth, as the guest of Martha and Mary, as the visitor at the Cana feast, He taught men that His religion is that of home, the religion of husband and wife, of brother and sister, of little children and their parents. With His dying words He confirmed this teaching, " Behold thy son . . . behold thy mother." Never since the commandment had been given, " Honour thy father and thy mother," amid the fires and thunders of Sinai, had it been so beautifully interpreted.

Surely these words of Jesus ought to teach us the sanctity of the home circle, and remind us that by taking our flesh Jesus became our Brother, a member of our family, and that therefore our home ought to be holy for His sake. Whether our home life is what it ought to be, our own consciences must tell us. Whether we act or speak as in the presence of our Brother Jesus, Who has marked home life with His Cross, and made it holy, our hearts must answer.

There is one part of domestic life to which our Lord's words specially refer—the relation of parents and children to each other. The life of Jesus is our perfect example in this as in all other things.

"He went down to Nazareth, and was subject unto them." He, their Master and their God. In His last hour, with all the agonies of crucifixion, and the still greater mental agony of bearing in His own sinless Person the sins of all men, Jesus thought of His mother and His friend. It is one of the significant signs of the day that the bond of union between parents and children is not what it once was. There is not the same love and reverence and deference to the parents' wishes on the part of the children. The selfishness of a pushing, crowding age, shows itself very strongly in the matter. Parents too often seem only anxious to get their children off their hands, and launched in the crowd; and children seem to resent the restraint and rules of home life. There was a time when the wish of a parent was law, next to the law of God, in the eyes of sons and daughters. Now-a-days children too often wish to be "a law unto themselves."

True love is perfectly unselfish, "seeketh not her own." And this love is alone found in Christ. He alone can make men to be of one mind in a house. Much of the so-called affection of the world is mere animalism, and is utterly selfish. True love is sanctified by Jesus, signed with His Cross, beautified by His example. We find it in the self-sacrifice of the parent for the welfare of the child, in the willing obedience of the children to the parent.

Blessed Jesu, Who in Thy dying moments didst provide a home for Thy mother, sanctify our home life, ·purify it from all selfishness and evil temper, and make our households fit for Thy sacred Presence.

XXXVIII.
Thursday in Holy Week.

THE SEVEN WORDS.—IV., V.

S. MATT. XXVII. 46.
"My God, My God, why hast Thou forsaken Me?"
S. JOHN XIX. 28.
"I thirst."

AFTER the third word was spoken from the Cross, there were silence and darkness at Calvary. From the sixth to the ninth hour—that is, from twelve to three o'clock—a supernatural gloom fell upon the scene. The darkness of midnight was present at mid-day! Silence reigned around the three crosses. Even the tongues of the busy mockers were still. The darkness hid the dying agonies of the Crucified, and a greater darkness concealed the agony of our Saviour's soul.

At last the silence was broken by an awful cry, mysterious, wonderful—" My God, My God, why hast Thou forsaken Me." The same words had been spoken long ago by David in his hour of darkness; but they had a deeper meaning now. What they meant fully we may not know, we dare not ask. The darkness is still there, the veil is between us and the true meaning.

The cry was the utterance of a breaking heart. It marks the very height of our Lord's agony. Crushed by physical pain, and in the very throes of death, the human nature of Jesus seemed to sink and fail beneath the burden. He Who was despised and rejected of men, seemed as if forsaken of God.

These feelings of intense depression are liable to come upon all of us at certain times, and in these seasons we have the comfort of knowing that Jesus sympathizes, since His soul was exceedingly sorrowful, even unto death, and He for a brief moment felt utter loneliness, as if no one cared for His soul.

But there was another reason for that sad cry of our Master's. He was suffering in the place of sinners—" The Father made Him to be sin for us, and He hath redeemed us from the curse of the law, being made a curse for us." Therefore all the suffering for sin, all the curse of sin, was laid upon the sinless Jesus, and the chief part of the punishment of sin is the hiding away of God's Face. So the Lord, Who is without sin, felt in His human nature the awful loneliness of those whose sin has shut them out from God. He must indeed tread the winepress *alone*. God hath laid upon Him the iniquity of us all. Dare we think or speak lightly of sin, when sin forced that bitter cry from the sinless lips of Jesus Christ?

When we feel forsaken, lonely, uncared for, let us turn for comfort to Him Who suffered the desolation of the Cross. He knows this sorrow, and He has promised, "I will never leave thee, nor forsake thee." Sometimes, when our prayers are not answered at once, we are tempted to think that God has forsaken us. We are inclined to say, "O my God, I cry in the day-time, but Thou hearest not, and in the night season also I take no rest." But as a Saint of God says wisely (S. Gregory), "Let no one, when he is not instantly heard, believe that he is neglected by the Divine care. For it often happens that our desires are heard on this very account, because they are not granted at once; and that which we wish to be fulfilled instantly, sometimes prospers the better for its very tardiness. Our cry is often granted by means of its being delayed, as the longer the grain is in sprouting above the earth, the larger is the crop which it brings forth."

"I thirst." The last words from the Cross were caused by agony of soul; this cry was the result of bodily torture. One of the worst parts of the pain of crucifixion is an intolerable, burning thirst. It was only just at the end that Jesus thought and spoke of Himself. First, His thoughts were for His enemies, then for the dying robber beside Him, then for His mother. What a contrast to us! We so often put self first, and afterwards, long afterwards, we think of others.

"I thirst." He thirsts—He, the Living Water, Who said, "Whosoever drinketh of the water that I shall give him shall never thirst." He thirsts—Who is the smitten Rock from which the healing waters flow. He thirsts—Who said by the mouth of His prophet, "Ho, every one that thirsteth, come ye to the waters; yea, come, buy wine and milk without money and without price." He—the Fountain opened on that day to the House of David, and to the inhabitants of Jerusalem, for sin and for uncleanness; He Who was on the Cross "a place of broad rivers and streams;" He Who said by His prophet, "I am poured out like water."

"He thirsts." Some kind hand, perhaps that of some secret disciple, gives Jesus a sponge dipped in vinegar. That was the only sign of mercy towards Him Who was dying to obtain mercy for all sinners. Again had our Lord fulfilled the Scriptures—"When I was thirsty, they gave me vinegar to drink."

Still, in one sense, our Lord in glory says, "I thirst." He thirsts for the love of men, for the salvation of souls; as the hart desireth the water-brooks, so longeth the soul of Jesus for His redeemed. As a tender parent yearns and longs for his children to grow up pure, and good, and noble, so yearns Jesus over us His children. He thirsts that we may thirst for Him; when we thirst for Him in a barren and dry land where no water is, we learn to minister to Him by helping others, as He said, "In that ye have done it unto the least of these ye did it unto Me."

Blessed Jesu, Who didst suffer lonely agony for our sins, teach us to hate sin, make us ever to thirst after righteousness, and evermore give us of the water of life freely.

XXXIX.
Good Friday.

THE SEVEN WORDS.—VI., VII.

S. JOHN XIX. 30.
"It is finished."
S. LUKE XXIII. 46.
"Father, into Thy Hands I commend My Spirit."

"IT is finished!" What a world of meaning is there in that one word, for it was but one in the language in which Jesus spoke. The life of earthly suffering was finished. The homeless Jesus, Who had nowhere to lay His Head, was to find rest in the rich man's tomb. The Body, once wrapped in coarse swaddling clothes, shall have Joseph's fine linen and Mary's spices. Angels shall guard it; and so the words are fulfilled—"His rest shall be glorious!"

Finished now the agony, the fasting, the temptation, the obedient childhood, the laborious youth, the patient years of labour; all finished now. Finished, too, is the work which His Father had given Him to-day. As a Child, the Lord had said, "Wist ye not that I must be about My Father's business?" Now He had finished the work which His Father had given Him to do. He had been obedient unto death, even the death of the Cross.

The work of redemption was finished, the work of example was complete. He had come to do His Father's will, and now—it is finished! Finished also is every prophecy or type of Scripture. The Seed of the woman has bruised the serpent's head; Jesus has been lifted up upon the Cross, as Moses lifted up the serpent in the wilderness; the Lamb of God has been sacrificed as our Passover, and not a bone of Him has been broken. The true Moses has ascended the Mount of the Cross, and stretched out His Hands that the battle with Satan may go on. The true Joshua has stretched forth His spear, never to be withdrawn till the enemy is conquered. The true Joseph has been sold and set at naught by His brethren, and is going into the Heavenly Goshen to prepare a place for them. The Scapegoat has borne the sins of the people—"It is finished!"

Jesus has made a perfect sacrifice of Himself—Body, Soul, and Will! He, the Second Adam, has paid the debt which the first Adam's sin had laid on all men. The gates of Paradise, once closed, are now open to all believers. He has purchased to Himself an universal Church at the price of His most precious Blood, He has provided it with a never-failing supply of grace, and has instituted Sacraments as the channels through which the grace may flow.

"It is finished!" Yes, Jesus finished His work; but our part remains. God gives to every man his work to be done. Daily we have to die unto sin and to rise again unto righteousness, daily we have to crucify our corrupt affections, daily we need the exercise of repentance and faith, daily we have a battle to fight, a race to run, looking unto Jesus, the Author and *Finisher* of our faith. Only when death calls us out of the strife shall we be able to say with truth, "Thanks be to God Who giveth us the victory through our Lord Jesus Christ—it is finished."

"Father, into Thy Hands I commend My Spirit." As Jesus had begun with the Father in His words from the Cross, so He ends with Him. Here is our example for every day. Let us begin and end each day with God, so that our life, our work, may be begun, continued, and ended in Him. Let us commit our spirit to God's keeping when we rise in the morning, and do all that we have to do in the Name of the Lord. Let us commend our spirit to God when we lie down to sleep, and we need fear no evil. Let us commend our spirit to God in the hour of death, as into the hands of a most merciful Father, and then we need to "dread the grave as little as our bed;" then whether we live, or whether we die, we shall be "for ever with the Lord."

Surely those dying words of Jesus rob death of its sting as far as Christ's people are concerned. Death comes to us as sweetly as God's kiss came to Moses and set free his soul. Death comes to us as a gentle nurse hushing her weary, wayward children to rest. We can lie down to die

> "As sweetly as a child,
> Whom neither thought disturbs
> Nor care encumbers,
>   Tired with long play
>   At close of summer's day,
> Lies down and slumbers."

Surely too, that sight of Jesus dead *for us* should deepen and strengthen our love for Him Who loved us and laid down His life for us. We sometimes fail to fully realize the love of some dear one till death has removed him from our sight. I well remember the agony of sorrow with which a daughter, standing by her mother's grave, cried out, "O my dear, dear mother." As we gaze for the last time on the dear dead face, we sometimes understand for the *first* time how deeply and truly we were loved. May it be so with us now as we gaze on the face of the Crucified. Perhaps, as it has been beautifully said, "When my sheep see me dead, they will know that it was love that killed me."

"Father, into Thy Hands I commend My Spirit." Well has it been said of these words, "O blessed verse, whereby the world's redemption was sealed, wherewith the most pure Spirit of the Saviour departed from His Most Sacred Body." This is the verse which, as it hallowed the dying bed of the Master, has formed the last utterance of many of His servants. Happy verse, which has merited to form the last accents of so many of those passing from death to life, from sorrow to joy, from a vale of misery to a Paradise of immortality. The proto-martyr ended his struggle with these words; the same words are recorded to have been uttered by the dying S. Nicholas, by S. Basil the Great, and by S. Louis of France, who with this prayer breathed forth his spirit on the coast of Tunis.

Let us try to learn this our lesson as we kneel before the silent Cross, to do the will of our Heavenly Father here on earth, to bear our cross, and then in faith and hope to commend our departing soul to the God Who gave it.

XL.
Easter Eve.

AT REST.

S. MATT. XXVII. 58.
"He went to Pilate, and begged the Body of Jesus."

AFTER darkness comes the light, after the storm the calm, after the battle peace, after hard labour rest. So was it with Jesus. The noise and confusion of Good Friday have given place to the sweet calm of Easter Eve.

The crowds have gone home, the crosses on Calvary stand dark and bare. And Jesus has found rest. Joseph, the rich councillor, has begged the Body of Jesus from Pilate, and aided by Nicodemus, the Lord's secret disciple, has laid the Body taken of a Virgin Mother in a virgin tomb. He Who was to be the first-fruits of them that slept, sleeps in a tomb wherein never man lay as yet. The weary Head with the scars of the thorny crown rests on a stone; the tortured limbs are easy now; He had gone forth to His work and to His labour until the evening, and now "it is finished." Now are the words fulfilled, "God rested on the seventh day from all His work." Now "the little hills may rejoice on every side," for Jesus lies among "the grassy barrows of the happier dead," and the little hillocks of the churchyard have a new and blessed meaning.

Even now the Scriptures are being fulfilled—"He was with the rich in His death." Two men of wealth and power among the Jews, Joseph and Nicodemus, are drawn by the power of the Cross. Nicodemus, who had been afraid to acknowledge himself a disciple openly whilst Jesus lived, is made brave by the power of the Cross to confess Christ crucified. The Spirit of Jesus was still working for the souls of His people; His Body was to rest, but His Spirit was with those spirits in prison—the spirits of just men— now to be made perfect by His redemption. Thus on all sides the Cross is beginning to draw men. The Centurion has confessed that Jesus is verily the Son of God; Joseph and Nicodemus are brought from the midst of His enemies, the Jewish Council, to be His followers; the penitent thief has passed into the promised Paradise, and has listened in company with Patriarch, and Priest, and Prophet to the wondrous story of salvation.

Everything on Easter Eve speaks of rest. The Body of Jesus rests in the rock-hewn tomb, the Soul of Jesus rests in peace where the wicked cease from troubling. The Church has always looked on this season as a type of the quiet time of rest between death and the resurrection. But for whom does this rest remain? For the people of God, for those to whom to live is Christ, and therefore to die is gain. We must live with Christ, we must suffer with Him, we must be buried with Him, if through the grave and gate of death we are to pass to our joyful resurrection.

If during this Lent we have tried to follow in the steps of Jesus, "glad with Him to suffer pain;" if God in His mercy has given us new and contrite hearts, hewn out of the rocky, stony heart of old, as a place where Jesus may come and with us continually dwell, then the coming Easter will indeed be a blessed Festival to us; when He Who sits upon the Throne will make all things new for us. If we would rise to higher, holier, purer lives, we must, like Joseph of Arimathæa, beg the Body of Jesus. He begged the Body of the dead Jesus that he might treasure it with loving hands, and minister to Him dead, Who living, came not to be ministered unto, but to minister. He brought fine linen for Him Who had been stripped by cruel hands, Whose garments his enemies had parted among them. He brought myrrh in token of His burial, even as the Wise Men had brought it long ago.

We, too, must draw near very early on this blessed Easter morning, and bring with us the fair white linen of penitence, and the sweet-smelling spices of our praise and thanksgivings. We must bring new and contrite hearts where the risen Jesus may find a resting-place. Humbly and devoutly, feeling our own utter unworthiness, we must beg the Body of Jesus, that our sinful bodies may be made clean by His Body, and our souls washed in His most precious Blood, and that we may evermore dwell in Him, and He in us.

Thus at the Altar of the Blessed Sacrament the risen Jesus will meet us, saying, "All hail!" Then let our prayer be, "We would see Jesus; Create in us a clean heart, O God, and renew a right spirit within us."

The true time of our rest and of our rising is not yet. It is not till we can say with truth, "I have finished the work that Thou gavest me to do," that the permission will be given, "Sleep on now, and take your rest." The battle, and the heat and burden of the day, and the watch and the prayer, and the agony and the Cross, must come before the rest of Easter Eve, and the glorious resurrection unto eternal life.

"Let us therefore *labour* to enter into that rest!" We may not understand much of the mystery of our life, the mystery of our sorrows, but God knoweth best.

> "If we could push ajar the gates of life,
>   And stand within, and all God's workings see,
> We could interpret all this doubt and strife,
>   And for each mystery could find a key,
> But not to-day. Then be content, poor heart!
>   God's plans, like lilies pure and white, unfold;
> We must not tear the close-shut leaves apart—
>   Time will reveal the calyxes of gold.
> And if, through patient toil, we reach the land
>   Where tired feet, with sandals loosed, may rest,
> Where we shall clearly see and understand—
>   I think that we shall say—'God knew the best.'"

THE END.

www.ingramcontent.com/pod-product-compliance
Lightning Source LLC
Chambersburg PA
CBHW030351170426
43202CB00010B/1332